"COMPEL THEM TO COME IN"

by Evangelist John R. Rice

copyright, 1961, by
Sword of the Lord Foundation

Price $2.00

D. Edmond Hiebert Collection

SWORD OF THE LORD FOUNDATION
Wheaton, Illinois

printed in U. S. A.

Contents

CHAPTER	PAGE
1. "Compel Them to Come In"	3
2. "The Fatherhood of God" and "The Brotherhood of Man"	15
3. The Double Curse of Booze	33
4. Dangerous Triplets	57
5. The Lord Our Righteousness	77
6. Father, Mother, Home, and Heaven	95
7. Serve God Without Regard for Consequences	117
8. The Blessings of Trouble	131
9. Will God Dwell With Men on the Earth?	147

"Compel Them to Come In"

(Message to Sunday School teachers and officers of Highland Park Baptist Church, Detroit, Michigan, September 12, 1948. Mechanically recorded for THE SWORD OF THE LORD.)

"Then said he unto him, A certain man made a great supper, and bade many: And sent his servant at supper time to say to them that were bidden, Come; for all things are now ready. And they all with one consent began to make excuse. The first said unto him, I have bought a piece of ground, and must needs go and see it: I pray thee have me excused. And another said, I have bought five yoke of oxen, and I go to prove them: I pray thee have me excused. And another said, I have married a wife, and therefore I cannot come. So that servant came, and shewed his Lord these things. Then the master of the house being angry said to his servant, Go out quickly into the streets and lanes of the city, and bring in hither the poor, and the maimed, and the blind. And the servant said, Lord, it is done as thou has commanded, and yet there is room. And the Lord said unto the servant, Go out into the highways and hedges, and compel them to come in, that my house may be filled. For I say unto you, That none of those men which were bidden shall taste of my supper."—Luke 14:16-24

Notice particularly verses 21 and 23: "So that servant came, and shewed his lord these things. Then the master of the house being angry said to his servant, Go out quickly into the streets and lanes of the city, and bring in hither the poor, and the maimed, and the halt, and the blind . . . And the lord said unto the servant, Go out into the highways and hedges, and compel them to come in, that my house may be filled."

Going After Sinners Is the Main Duty of Christians

Sunday School teachers need to learn to compel people to be saved, compel people to come to Sunday School, compel them to listen to the Bible, compel them to get converted. It may sound impossible, but when you remember that Jesus Christ is the One who said it, then you know that we can compel them to come in.

In this parable which Jesus gave are a great many of the difficulties that a soul winner meets. Yet He still commands us to go and get them. Jesus says that many will lie about it. Some will say, "I know it is night, but I must see some ground; I've already bought it, but I must see it tonight at supper time." Somebody else will say, "I bought five yoke of oxen. I have not tried them yet, but tonight at supper time I am going to hitch them up and break them in." Another will say, "I've married a wife and so cannot come." Now, all of those are silly excuses.

People today make silly excuses. Some will make alibis, some will lie; some will turn it down. Yet Jesus plainly says, "That is all right; you go and get them! If you work you can get some people. If you cannot get one you can get another. Go ahead." Analyze what Jesus said here and you find that the main thing for a Christian is to go. He "said to his servant, Go out quickly into the streets and lanes of the city, and bring in hither the poor, and the maimed, and the halt, and the blind."

The servant came back and said, "I've done what you said and there is some more room."

"Have you been all over town—down the main streets, in the back alleys and lanes of the city?"

"Yes."

"All right, then, go out into the country and compel them to come in that My house may be filled."

The main thing about soul winning is to go after people. Somebody says, "Well, I just don't have the talent." No, that is not the main thing. You do not have the gumption and the get-up. That is all! It is not talent you need. Mainly it is faithfulness enough to go and do what God said to do, what Jesus Christ commanded. Anybody who will work at it can win souls because that is the main thing. Jesus said to go, to work at it.

This is what the Bible says everywhere else. In Psalm 126:6 the Scripture says: "He that goeth forth . . ." The first thing to do about soul winning is to go. In the Great Commission Jesus said: "All power is given unto me in heaven and in earth. Go ye therefore . . ." And in Mark 16:15 the Lord put it in these words: "Go ye into all the world, and preach the gospel . . ." The *go* is before preaching. The *go* is before teaching. The *go* is before baptizing. The going is the main thing. You did not fail in the teaching so much. You are likely to fail more in the going. That is the way it is.

Follow the example of New Testament Christians and you will find that the main thing they did was to go. They were not extraordinary men. Peter was a fisherman. Levi was a common tax collector. James and John were fishermen, and Andrew. They were ordinary people—uneducated, more or less. In fact, we are told in the book of Acts that "when they saw . . that they were unlearned and ignorant men, they marvelled and took knowledge of them . . ." They just turned the world upside down, yet they were ignorant and unlearned men. They did what Jesus said: they went. Now, listen to me people; you teachers get this on your hearts: "I can go and get people for Jesus." That is the main thing a Christian ought to do. Your burden ought to be, "I must get people for Jesus! I can go and fill up my class. I can get them to Jesus Christ. That is what He commanded me to do!"

Some people have the idea that the main thing God requires is that you be a good talker. Oh, if you can just have the gift of gab! Oh, if you can just put it over on the people; if you can just turn on your magnetism and personality and shine! But that is not what the Lord says. All a good servant had time to do was to hotfoot it from one place to another and say, "You are invited, you remember. Will you be there tonight?"

Then he would come back and report: "I told them and a lot of them said they would not come."

"All right, then, go out quickly into the streets and lanes of the city. Get a move on. Step on it! You are too slow—go ahead!"

He would report back again and say, "I've done everything you told me and yet there is room."

"Have you been to every lane and street in town?"

"Yes."

"Well, then, go out into the country, in the highways and the hedges and to the creek bottoms. Go and compel them to come in!"

Now what I am trying to lay on your heart is that God's plan for soul winning is primarily to go after people. God intends for Christians to go get people saved.

Difficulties Need Not Prevent You From Winning Souls

Now, second, there are difficulties—certainly! But there are not any difficulties that can keep you from winning somebody. This servant went to one man and said, "I want you to come; you are invited."

The fellow said, "I have bought some ground; I am bound to go and see it tonight."

Another fellow said, "I've bought some oxen."

Another said, "I'm married." Well, you know even if a man is married he can still go to church. A man who is married can still be saved. A man who is married can still take his wife out to dinner. You are going to meet objections. You are going to meet alibis. You are going to have some disappointments. You will not get everybody. But if you cannot win one, go and get another one. There is always somebody you can get.

In Dallas two women, Mrs. Middleton and Mrs. Crawford, one time went to do soul winning. They went down Tenth Street where there were many nice houses, a lovely residence district, the nicest in our end of town. Up and down the street they went. When they came back they were so discouraged! "Well," they said, "we did win one woman, a maid. Nearly always we were met at the door by a maid. The maid would say, 'Madam doesn't have time to talk to you today,' or 'She is out,' or something else. Most of the time we couldn't even get into the house. In a few cases we got to talk to the colored maid, but that was all. We have walked until our feet are sore—we have walked half a day—and we have won just one soul."

"Well," I said, "if you won just one soul and could do that every half day, hallelujah! That would be over seven hundred in a year's time! And if you could keep one soul out of Hell for a million years by a half a day's work, why that would be wonderful. You shouldn't feel bad about that! But if you cannot win one, try another. Did they turn you down? All right, go down here on Elm Street, down by the park where there are a lot of little shotgun houses on little twenty-five foot lots. [The houses had rooms right behind each other because they did not have room to spread out any other way.] Go down there. The maid will not come to the door, because they do not have any maid. The Madam will not say she is busy, because nearly all of them are on relief and the whole family will be at home. They go down on the railroad track and pick up a few extra pieces of coal that fall off the coal cars in the wintertime."

I knew how it was because I had been down there just a few nights before to take a pair of shoes to a girl so she could come to Sunday School. They called in the neighbors next door and said, "Wait, Brother Rice, you and Mrs. Rice sit down." They went and got the neighbors on either side and said, "Brother Rice is over at our house. Come over and hear him talk." And they got the whole house full of people for me to preach to.

So I said, "They won't run you off. You may not win the hoity-toity and the up-and-outs. But down there where they are poor, where they are on relief, where their floors are uncovered, where they do not get to go to church much because they have only shabby clothes and are tickled because a preacher pays them some attention—I say those people will listen to you." Listen! You can always get somebody. You cannot win everybody; but, thank God, you can win somebody. If you cannot get one, go and get another.

Here is a wonderful thing; it is the plan throughout the Bible. Paul would go somewhere to preach and they would kick him out of the synagogue. So he got used to getting kicked out. He would preach the best he could and get a few Jews converted, then they would kick him out and he would go to the Gentiles. He would go right next door to the synagogue and start a meeting. He would go first to the Jews and win some. Then there would come a row and a big fight. Maybe he would get beaten or put in jail, or stoned. Then he would preach to the Gentiles. He went over to Rome and talkĕd to those people. Some of them were converted and some were not. Some started trouble and Paul said, "Lo, I turn to the Gentiles." He said, "I am debtor both to the Greeks, and to the Barbarians; both to the wise, and to the unwise" (Rom. 1:14). If he could not get Jews, he got Gentiles. If he could not get the up-and-outs, he got the down-and-outs. Go and get them!

I love this noble church and your fine pastor. But do you know one danger? You people are so nice that you are likely to get to where you do not care for people who do not have their faces washed. You are likely to get to where you do not think so much of the people who cannot dress up for Sunday. If you do not watch your step you will be sinning against God. You will get so smart and hoity-toity that you will not pay any attention to the halt and the lame and the blind. Jesus said, "If you can't get these people who were invited first, go and get the poor and the lame and the halt and the blind. If they will not hear you, get out into the country and get the country people, then." You can always get somebody. If you cannot get the ones you wanted first, get somebody else.

I remember in my boyhood home a Mrs. Smith. She had been praying for years for her husband. When revival meeting time came on she would say, "I want you people to pray for Jot. I am so burdened for Jot, my husband." One day she got up and said, "I had it out with God last night. I told God, 'All right—if you save my husband, well and good; but I am not going to let everybody else go to Hell while I pray for my husband. I am going out and get somebody who is interested in being saved.'" You can always find somebody. That is the reason for the house-to-house visitation. That is the reason for running people down. Go and get them!

Many Can Be Won Whom You Think Are Too Hard

Notice another thing: it is quite evident from the story here that if you only go you will find a lot of people who can be won whom you thought were too hard. You just thought you could not do it. Everywhere I go, Christian people have marked off a lot of people. They have said, "Now we can't win the Jews and we can't win the Catholics. And that other man—there is no use talking to him. He is an infidel. Here is another fellow; he is a drunkard —you can't win him. This other man doesn't like preachers—he just cusses preachers!" The first thing you know you have trimmed yourself down to a handful of children. And you let the rest of the world go to Hell. You ought to be ashamed. Listen to me! There are more people you could win if you ever made up your mind to it.

I know what you say here in Detroit. "The people are so worldly and there are so many churches." Yes, I know; but after I preached this morning and before I could get down to talk to the Sunday School class, I met in the aisle a fine Catholic young man, and talked to him. A young woman who is here was talking to him. I talked to him, too, and made clear the plan of salvation. We prayed together, he trusted Christ and happily claimed the Lord. His father who was a backslider, came back and promised God and me he would be responsible for the boy and lead him on for the Lord. If you will pay any attention, you just stumble over people you can win.

Then I talked to the class and before I could get out of there, here came a twelve-year-old girl to meet her dad and mother who were in the class. She is in the seventh grade. She is nobody's fool. She is not just a little bit of a kid; her body is taking on the form of womanhood. She already frizzles her hair, and is thinking about the boys. She, I found, had never been converted. In five minutes' time I won her to Christ.

What I am saying is that they are all about you, but you do not go after them. You could win people if you really tried. You could! People say, "Oh, you can't win Catholics." I beg your pardon. Thank God, I know, I win them, many of them. I know better than that. I won hundreds of Catholics and Jews. You can win Jews. We had a Jewish woman saved Friday night.

Some years ago I was in a tent meeting in downtown Brooklyn, right by the big Y. M. C. A. Grace, my daughter, had children's meeting. More little Italian boys and girls and Greek children and Slovaks came. She got a great crowd of Jews and Catholics. That was nearly all there were in that area. She said, "These are from Catholic and Jewish families and I must be tactful; I must take it easy." So she told them Bible stories, taught them little choruses, tried to win their friendship; but she did not press the matter of salvation, because she did not want to drive anybody away. The second and third days she did the same. About the fourth day she finally told them about sin, told them that all were sinners and were lost forever if they did not have Jesus, and urged them to turn to the Lord Jesus to save them. She said "How many here know you are sinners?" The whole bunch of them knew they were sinners. "Well," she said, "God loves you and Jesus died for you Don't you think you ought to come to Him?"

"Yes," they said.

"All right, we'll just ask Jesus to save you right now." And when they had their prayer, one by one these Jewish and Catholic children said they would take Christ as Saviour. A boy ten or eleven years old said, "Why, Miss Grace, listen! this is the most important thing in the world. Isn't it strange that none of us thought of this the first day?" Wasn't that a rebuke?

You go all around Robin Hood's barn about the matter when people are about to die and go to Hell. Don't you think people have any sense? Don't you think they have any conscience? Don't you think they know they have to meet God? Don't you think they know they are sinners? And you think you can't win Catholics! You could win them all the time if you tried.

I preached in Chicago "A Sermon From a Catholic Bible" and we had twenty-four professions that night—about half of them Catholics. Some of them follow me around when I go back to Chicago for a meeting. I was in a meeting out at Lawndale Bible Church the other day and a man and his wife came to hear me. They are members of the Moody Church and came all the way across Chicago, twelve or fifteen miles, to hear me preach because she had been a Catholic and was saved there in May two years ago. She said, "You don't remember me, do you? I was saved when you preached 'A Sermon From a Catholic Bible' out at the big Arena in Chicago. Oh, we will never forget you." You can win Jews and Catholics!

I am saying that there are many people you do not have any idea you could win but whom you could win if you went after them. Far more people have hungry hearts than you dream of.

After I attended Southwestern Seminary I was out in the pastorate some years. Then Mrs. Rice and I came back and built a home on Seminary Hill in Fort Worth where the Southwestern Seminary is located. My wife attended the seminary church, the Gambrell Street Baptist Church, where she was in a Sunday School class with a hundred other women. It was taught by Mrs. L. R. Scarborough, the wife of the famous president of the Southwestern Seminary, a great evangelist and wonderful soul winner. At least half the women in the class, I suppose, were wives of preachers or wives of missionaries. Some of them were wives of the seminary faculty, others were wives of seminary students, others were wives of the missionaries, etc.

In the class there was one unsaved woman. My wife said to me one time when I came in from a meeting: "Dear, I am troubed about a woman in my class. There are a hundred women in the class and only one of them unsaved She is there every Sunday. I suppose everybody has talked to her She must be gospel-hardened. I don't know that we could do anything with her; yet I feel we ought to try. Would you go with me to see her?"

I said, "Yes, I'll go." We prayed a good deal about it. It was bound to be a tough case, we felt. She was bound to be gospel-hardened. She lived ony two doors below Dr. Scarborough. A preacher lived on one side of her and a Christian educational worker on the other side. We felt that everybody surely had talked to her so much that she was hardened. So we hired a woman to come and spend a half day with the children. We felt, "This is going to be a hard fight. It will be a long, hard pull!" The woman came to stay with the children and we went over to the unsaved woman's house.

We knocked on the door, and with fear and trembling watched the door open. But the woman instead of throwing hot water on us, said, "Why, Mrs. Rice, I'm glad to see you; come in! Is this Brother Rice?" (Down South all preachers are "brothers," you know.) We went inside. I wanted to talk to her about her soul but I felt "She must be so tough and hard that I must find some easy way to slip up on her"— you know, sort of bring the conversation around. We are so tactful sometimes, you know, that we never make contact!

I saw a lovely Bible and I thought, "Well, now I can talk to her about that Bible." I said "Say, this certainly is a nice Bible you have here."

"Yes," she said, "my mother gave me that last Christmas. I am very proud of it."

"That is fine. I understand that

you are not a Christian, but if you were a Christian wouldn't it be fine? You and your husband could read some in this Bible every night before you go to bed. You could read it and have a good time. Wouldn't that be nice?"

"Well," she said, "but we already read it every night. Ever since Mother gave it to us last Christmas my husband and I have read a chapter every night."

Well, that rather took the wind out of my sails. So I started again. "But if you were a Christian you could get down here and have prayer, ask God to keep you through the night, thank Him for the blessings of the day and talk to your heavenly Father. Wouldn't it be nice if you were a Christian?"

By this time there were tears in her eyes and she said, "But we do pray every night. We read a chapter in the Bible, and then he gets down by his chair and I get down by my chair here, and we pray. We have been doing that every night since last Christmas."

I finally got bold enough to just come out with the thing plainly, and I said, "Well, why aren't you saved?"

She began to sob like a little child—and sobbed and sobbed. "I want to be saved. I have done everything I know. We read the Bible. We pray every night. I don't know how!"

"Well," I said, "God bless you, you are sure going to find out how!" I took that new Bible that she had been reading every day, turned to the third chapter of John and showed her how God loved her, how Jesus died for her and how that if she would put her trust in Jesus He would save her in five minutes she was a happy Christian. Every Sunday morning she had been sitting in that Bible class with a hundred women, all of them Christians and half of them preachers wives, and nobody had ever told her how to be saved, nobody had ever gone to see her and talk to her about it, nobody ever encouraged her to come to Jesus, nobody ever told her how, when she and her poor husband were living there in a home in the midst of preachers and Christian workers! What I am saying is that you can win souls. There are plenty of people you can win. But you do not work at it; you do not go after them!

The Saviour here says for you to go out and *compel* them to come in. "Go out into the highways and hedges, and compel them to come in, that my house may be filled." The Saviour is taking for granted that you are not to mind about the difficulties. There are plenty of people you can get.

Anybody Who Really Works At It Can Win Souls

Now, there is another thing that I want you to see: anybody can do it. I am so glad the Lord has business that fits anybody who is willing to be faithful. You do not have to be brilliant. There are some who feel: "Now if you want something extra special—and in public, of course, where everybody will know it and where I will get applause—I will do it. But this drudgery of getting out and pushing doorbells and trudging from house to house, hard work like that—well, my talents are so great I can't do that."

A woman wrote to me and said she felt sure God wanted her to be a preacher. I said, "All right, get busy with your own family and your loved ones who are not saved."

"Oh," she said, "but with my talents I think God wants me to preach in public." She did not win her own children, did not win her next-door neighbors; but she thought she ought to put on a big show with her talents. The Lord Jesus isn't primarily concerned about talent. If it comes to ability, He has it already. If it comes to money, He already has it. The cattle on a thousand hills are His. The gold and silver are His. If He were hungry, He would not ask you. No, what you can give is the kind of devotion that gets out and puts your foot in your hand, as the old saying down South goes, and go after it. Just hotfoot it from door to door! Talk to one and then another. If they turn you down, go to some more, go with a broken heart—but keep going! Anybody can do it!

I wish you knew some of the soul winners I have known. I am thinking now about Hillus Gass in Dallas, Texas. God bless him! Someone from there told us the other day that Hillus Gass was still going. For a time he was sick and they expected him to die. Now he has arthritis so bad that he can just barely shuffle along. But he gives out tracts and stops people and talks to them. He is unprepossessing. He came from a very poor family. He wears thick-lensed glasses. Besides that he is abrupt in speech.

One time I was with him and some young fellows came along. He said, "Wait, Brother Rice, I want to talk to these boys." He said, "Here, boys, wait; I want to give you a tract." Then he asked each one of them if he were a Christian. They told him no, and he said, "Well, you are going to Hell then, aren't you?"

They said, "Well we guess so; we hadn't thought about it."

I remember when we had the Texas Centennial he wanted to go out to the fair. I thought he would get tired of that. But he would work a little, rake up some money and go for a day. Then he would work some more and go out again. All day long he would give out tracts, talk about the Lord and get people saved. He would say, "Boy, I wish I could do this every day." But he would have to go to work a little more and make enough money to pay his way for another day or two. Finally his brother-in-law said, "Listen, Hillus, I'm not much good at this. But I'll board you if you can go out there."

"All right," he said, "if I can just get a season ticket."

I told him I would pay $15.00 for a season ticket. And boy, was he in heaven! Brother W. E. Hawkins paid for a ticket for Charles Cline and they went out there all day every day. There was a girl show, so Brother Hillus went down there and talked to some of the girls. People would pay so much to see the carnival— to see the girls do their little

11

dances, sing their little songs, and so on. A Jew came along and said, "Hey, you will ruin my business talking about Jesus Christ."

"Are you a Christian?"

"No; I'm a Jew."

"Well, wait a minute! You will go to Hell if you don't get Jesus Christ."

"Well, but I . . ."

"No, listen to what the Bible says . . ." And the Jew could hardly get away from him. So somebody else called a policeman.

The policeman said, "Here, you are disturbing people."

Brother Hillus Gass said, "I have a season pass; here is my ticket. Why can't I talk to anybody I want to?"

"Well, but you are causing trouble," he said.

Brother Hillus said, "Listen, officer, are you a Christian?"

"Oh, no," he said, "I-I . . ."

"But wait a minute, officer . . ." And if he didn't get that policeman converted! When the summer was over those two boys brought me a list of over five hundred who claimed Christ. They spent all day every day working at it. I say this man was the most unprepossessing person. I say as ordinary and unlettered and unmagnetic as he was, yet he worked at it.

The best soul winners I know have not been educated people.

There was Mrs. Hardesty in Dallas, a seamstress who had only a high school education. She had never gone to a Bible school. She had never even taught a Sunday School class. Yet she got on fire to win souls and began to win them. One day, the twenty-fifth day of June, 1933, she promised God she would try to win a hundred souls by Christmas; and she won 151 or 152. Then the next year she set out to try to win 500. The year went by and on New Year's Night she got up to confess her sins before God. She said, "Brother Rice, I didn't win 500. I could have if I had meant business as I ought to have. I only won 360." A lot of preachers preach ten years and do not get that many saved. She worked at it day and night. What it takes is going after the people! Anybody can be a soul winner.

With Holy Fervor and the Power of the Holy Spirit We Can Compel Sinners to Be Saved

And the last word I must say is that we are to compel them. You say, "Can I make a person be saved?" Yes, sometimes you can. You are to compel them to come in.

I heard Gypsy Smith preach in Dallas one time. I determined before God that I was going to talk to the first man I saw about his soul. So when I got outside the church there was a taxi driver waiting beside the curb. I said, "Say, listen; I want to talk to you. Are you saved?"

"Yes, sir, I believe I am."

I said, "Are you sure you have been born again?"

"Yes, I believe I have," he said.

I said, "Well, when did it happen?"

"Just now. There was a little short man with gray mustache who came out the side door here (in the late Dr. Truett's church, the First Baptist Church, Dallas). He talked to me. He said, 'You dare not wait! You may go to Hell tonight.' He seemed so anxious that I felt I had to decide it now, and I did." Gypsy Smith had beat me to the taxi driver. You can get people saved. You can compel them to come in. You can compel them not only by teaching, by repetition and pressing the matter; but, listen, you can have the power of the Holy Spirit of God who works miracles, who makes drunkards sober and makes harlots pure. The miracle-working power of the Holy Spirit will go with you if you ever really mean business. Oh, may God give you that power that will help you to compel people to come in!

Let's go and compel them to come in! You Sunday School teachers are as accountable to God for bringing people in, getting them in your classes, as the superintendent is, or as the pastor is about the general congregation. Go and compel them to come in. Go and *bring* them in! You could have plenty of lost people here to preach to every Sunday, you would have them every Sunday coming to claim Christ, join the church and be baptized if you would just go and compel them to come in. God give you grace to do it!

"The Fatherhood of God" and "The Brotherhood of Man"

(SERMON PREACHED AT CENTRAL MANOR CAMP MOUNTVILLE, PENNSYLVANIA, AUGUST, 1952. MECHANICALLY RECORDED FOR THE SWORD OF THE LORD.)

". . . They which are the children of the flesh, these are not the children of God . . ."—Rom. 9:8.

"Ye do the deeds of your father. Then said they to him, We be not born of fornication; we have one Father, even God. Jesus said unto them, If God were your Father, ye would love me: for I proceeded forth and came from God; neither came I of myself, but he sent me. Why do ye not understand my speech? even because ye cannot hear my word. Ye are of your father the devil, and the lusts of your father ye will do. He was a murderer from the beginning, and abode not in the truth, because there is no truth in him. When he speaketh a lie, he speaketh of his own: for he is a liar, and the father of it."—John 8:41-44.

Jesus said, "After this manner therefore pray ye: Our Father which art in Heaven . . ." (Matt. 6:9). Now does Jesus mean that every person on earth is a child of God? Is God the Father of us all? Are all of us spiritually brothers? Those are serious questions and I will answer them tonight by God's grace from the Word of God.

I. The Fatherhood of God

First of all, tonight I speak on the Fatherhood of God. Is God the Father of all men on earth?

1. God Is the Father of Jesus Christ

A most important, wonderful truth for us is that God is literally the Father of our Lord Jesus Christ. When the angel came to Mary, as recorded in Luke, chapter 1 he said, "The Holy Ghost shall come upon thee, and...that holy thing which shall be born of thee shall be called the Son of God." Jesus is literally the Son of God. By a miracle, the Holy Spirit of God came upon a virgin girl, a woman who had no husband, a woman who knew not a man, and conceived in her womb this holy child Jesus. And Jesus came into this world a Son of God; a son of the woman, but not a son of any human father. By a miracle of

God, Jesus Christ was born; and He is God in person, and the Son of God

The Scripture takes this up in Hebrews, the first chapter.

> "God, who at sundry times and in divers manners spake in time past unto the fathers by the prophets, Hath in these last days spoken unto us by his Son ..."—Heb. 1:1,2a.

And again, verse 5,

> "For unto which of the angels said he at any time, Thou art my Son, [quotation from the second Psalm] this day have I begotten thee? And again, I will be to him a Father, and he shall be to me a Son?"

And that means Jesus is to be worshipped as God.
Verse 6 says,

> "And again, when he bringeth in the firstbegotten into the world, he saith, And let all the angels of God worship him."

Jesus Christ deserves worship as God, just as truly as the Father. In verse 8,

> "But unto the Son he saith, Thy throne, O God, is for ever and ever: a sceptre of righteousness is the sceptre of thy kingdom."

God the Father said to the Son "Thy throne, O God, is for ever and ever." Jesus Christ is God.

Back in Isaiah, the Scripture tells some words about the coming Saviour. And it is prophesied of Him,

> "For unto us a child is born, unto us a son is given: . . .and his name shall be called Wonderful, Counsellor, The mighty God, The everlasting Father, The Prince of Peace."—Isa. 9:6.

Jesus is "the mighty God." Jesus is God as much as the Father is God. Jesus is as worthy of worship as the Father is worthy of worship.

Jesus Christ has all judgment given into His hand. He will judge for the Father and instead of the Father.

Jesus is the Creator. We sometimes speak of God the Father as the Creator. That is a mistake, unless you mean that in the same sense that the Father and Son and Holy Spirit are one and all partake of it. The truth is, we are plainly told that God did all His creation through the hand of His Son. "All things were made by him, and without him was not anything made that was made" (John 1:3). Everything was made by the hand of Jesus Christ. The whole world began when Jesus was with God in the beginning. "In the beginning was the Word, and the Word was with God, and the Word was God. The same was in the beginning with God" (John 1:1,2).

Jesus Christ: *Jesus,* the human name; *Christ,* the divine and eternal name before the world began —Jesus was with the Father. He is the only begotten Son of God, has the same nature as God, is as good as God, as wise as God, as righteous as God, as holy as God, as merciful as God! He is the express image of the person of God (Heb. 1:3). When you pray to Jesus, you pray just like you pray to the Father. And He is as worthy of worship and praise, and in every sense partakes of everything that makes God deity. Jesus is the Son of God. Praise the Lord for that! Jesus Christ is the Son of God, our Father in Heaven. He is the Son of God—literally so.

Now we do sometimes hear people say that Jesus did not claim to be the Son of God. Nothing is clearer in the Bible than that He claimed to be the Son of God. For that, we are told that the Jews sought to slay Him because He claimed that God was His Father, and made Himself to be equal with God (John 5:18).

When the Jews said to Him, "Why, Abraham's dead. Why, do You mean that You are as old as Abraham?" Jesus answered, "Before Abraham was, I am" (John 8:58). What does He mean? He means that He is the God who appeared to Moses and said, 'Moses, go back and tell My people that I AM hath sent you' (Exod. 3:14). Jesus said, 'I am the One—I am the One who called Moses and spoke out of the burning bush. I am the One who created the world. I am the One who called Jacob back to start the nation Israel.' Jesus said, "I AM." Jesus is God. He is the only begotten of the Father. He is the unique Son of God, which means that He is the Son of God, not like other men are, but as no one else ever was or could be—Jesus, the Son of God. The first great fact about the Fatherhood of God is that He is the Father, in a unique sense, of our Lord Jesus Christ.

2. By Nature Men are Creatures of God But Not Children of God

The second thing the Bible teaches about the Fatherhood of God is that while He is the Creator of all men, He is not the Father of all men in any spiritual sense. Now men were all created by God. Back in Genesis, chapter 3, verse 20, "Adam called his wife's name Eve; because she was the mother of all living." That means that every man, woman, and child on the earth is descended from the same source, the same parents, the same Mother Eve.

Again over in I Corinthians, chapter 15, the Bible tells us plainly that "as in Adam all die." What does that mean? That means that every person here is descended from Adam, and so every person here has inherited the taint of Adam's sin. Every person in the world is full of sin. There are not several species of men in the world. There is one race of men as far as our source, our origin is concerned. Black man, white man, yellow man — everybody came from exactly the same source. Back from Noah and his three sons was the earth populated. And before then, from Adam. In Acts, chapter 17, verse 26, Paul is preaching at Athens in Greek. Paul says to the people that God "hath made of one blood all nations of men for to dwell on all the face of the earth." All the people in the world are of one blood.

Now men are made by God. Does that mean that all men are the children of God? There never was a more foolish statement, and it has been widespread everywhere, that all men are the children of God. All that can mean, to honest men who know the Bible, is that men are the creatures of God, are created of God.

You say, "I know that I'm a child of God because God created me." Then a cow is a child of God in exactly the same sense that you are, for God created the cow, too. If you mean we are creatures of God, that we are the offspring of God, that we are His invention, that He has the patent on us, that He made us, that He owns us—that is right. But you may own an automobile without it being your child. You may make a toy without it really being your child. God made men, that is true. But there is not any spiritual sense in which we are the children of God by nature. By nature men are not children of God.

What do I mean? I mean that the whole race of men is a fallen, sinful race. There is nothing in the Bible made clearer than this. The Bible says that "the heart is deceitful above all things, and desperately wicked. Who can know it?" In Isaiah 53:6 we read, "All we like sheep have gone astray; we have turned everyone to his own way..." In Romans, the third chapter, the Scripture says, "There is none righteous, no, not one... They are all gone out of the way, they are together become unprofitable; there is none that doeth good, no, not one," not one good person on the earth.

A man came to Jesus one time and said, "Good Master [the word he used was 'rabbi,' 'professor,' 'teacher'] what shall I do to inherit eternal life?"

Jesus answered, "Why callest thou me good? none is good, save one, that is, God."

Jesus did not mean He was not good. He meant, "If you think I'm good, don't call me 'rabbi.' Call me God Almighty in human form. Call me Son of God and Savior. Call me the pre-existent Christ. Call me what I am—the holy begotten of the Father. Don't call me 'rabbi' and say I'm good. If I'm just a rabbi, rabbis are not good. Professors are not good. Preachers are not good. Men are not good. I am God in human form. You can call me good if you call me God. There is none good but one—that is, God."

We had as well face the fact that the whole human race is a race of sinners, a fallen race, a degenerate race. Now let me say a word to my post-millennial friends, my a-millennial friends, all who are trying to correct the world, and trying to make the world a better place in which to live. Now I am for you when you try to put down sin. I am for you in trying to vote out liquor. I will tell you what I would do: I would vote out this socialistic, pro-communistic, this pink, red New Deal administration that has gotten its tentacles on common people, and bribing you with jobs and taking other men's money that they earned and giving it to you, to plow up crops, to keep you from earning money and to buy the votes of you farmers and buy the votes of you who labor. I would vote out this ungodly, heathen, New Deal, socialistic, pro-communistic gang. I am for making the world better.

But you had better face the fact that you are not going to make it all right. This world is doomed! The race of mankind is a wicked, fallen race, alien from God. Oh, what men need is new hearts! The only way we are ever going to fix this world for Jesus Christ is to have Him come in person and clean out the Devil-possessed sinners and take charge. Now this world is a bad world. If you have not found out that, then you are a babe in the woods.

3. Unconverted Sinners Are "Children of This World," "Children of Disobedience," "Children of Wrath," "Children of the Devil"

The Bible clearly teaches that all men by nature are sinners. We are not the children of God, but what the Bible calls unconverted people by nature, what the Bible calls "the children of this world" (Luke 16:8). The Devil is the god of this world. And lost sinners are "the children of this world."

What does the Bible call unsaved people? They are "the children of wrath" (Eph. 2:3). God is love. We who are the children of God, love God. God puts love in our hearts. So those who are the children of God are children of love. Those that are the children of the Devil are children of wrath. The lost world, unconverted people, are children of this world, children of wrath.

Unconverted people are "children of disobedience" (Eph. 2:2; Col. 3:6). Is not that what the Bible says again and again? Men are "by nature the children of wrath," by nature estranged from God, by nature strangers from God, by nature "dead in trespasses and in sin," spiritually dead. If you are unconverted, you are not akin to God, but akin to your father, the Devil. We are plainly told, in Romans 9:8, "...They which are the children of the flesh, these ARE NOT the children of God..."

Now that question came up with Jesus. Jesus talked one time to some people who claimed to be God's children. They had this idea of the universal Fatherhood of God. Jesus talked to the Pharisees. These people must have represented some of the leaders of the National Council of Churches. These people must have represented some of the bishops of all denominations joined in together. See what Jesus said to these people who believed in the universal Fatherhood of God and the brotherhood of man!

"And he said unto them, Ye are from beneath; I am from above: ye are of this world; I am not of this world."—John 8:23.

Now some people say, the modernists say, that Jesus was a good man, maybe even the best man who ever lived. But they say He had some deity in Him, and we have some deity in us. Modernist, you are a liar! You know you are not of God. Jesus said, "I am from above, you are from beneath. I am from God, you are not from God."

Now I read a little further,

> "I said therefore unto you, that ye shall die in your sins: for if ye believe not that I am he, ye shall die in your sins." —John 8:24.

Skip on down a few verses, down to verse 41. Jesus is speaking to the same people, the folks who drove Him to the cross, the folks who crucified Him. They were religious people who believed in the universal Fatherhood of God. The same people hate Jesus now if you press Him as the all-authoritative Saviour. If you press Him as the only way to God, if you say that everybody must bow the knee, if you say that Jesus is the virgin-born Saviour and the Judge of all the earth, and God in human form, that crowd that talks about the universal Fatherhood of God hate Him now!

Anybody who says that all men are by nature the children of God is trying to put Jesus down on the level of man, and put other men up on the level with Jesus Christ. It is a little Jesus and a big humanity. That is what the Devil's crowd, the modernists, want. Here is what Jesus said in verse 41:

> "Ye do the deeds of your father. Then said they to him, We be not born of fornication; we have one Father, even God."

See, they are claiming to be children of one father—God. "We have one Father," they said.

> "Jesus said unto them, If God were your Father, ye would love me: for I proceeded forth and came from God; neither came I of myself, but he sent me. Why do ye not understand my speech? even because ye cannot hear my word."—John 8:42, 43.

Lost man, you say, "That sounds like foolishness to me." That is right. That is because you are the Devil's child. You are not even spiritually alive and you do not have the Holy Ghost in you to teach you. You cannot even understand spiritual truth. Spiritual things are spiritually discerned. You are spiritually dead. You say, "I don't like that." You do not like that because you are not of God. Listen again.

> "Why do ye not understand my speech? even because ye cannot hear my word. Ye are of your father the devil, and the lusts of your father ye will do. He was a murderer from the beginning, and abode not in the truth, because there is no truth in him. When he speaketh a lie, he speaketh of his own: for he is a liar, and the father of it. And because I tell you the truth, ye believe me not. Which of you convinceth me of sin?"—John 8:43-46a.

Does anybody here want to take up that challenge yourself and say, "I can prove Jesus Christ sinned"? All right, do you give up? Well then, does anybody here want to stand up and say, "You cannot convince me of sin"? Give me a few minutes, brother, and I will give plenty of witnesses to that. Is your wife here? It would not take me long to do that. "But if I say the truth, why do you not believe me? He that is of God heareth God's word. Ye therefore hear them not because ye are not of

God." If you find anybody who does not believe the Bible, that man is not of God. That is the trouble. That is what Jesus said. Go back to verse 44, "Ye are of your father the devil." Who is this? Drunkards? Who is this? Harlots? Who is this? Criminals? These are church people. These are people circumcised the eighth day, bringing tithes into the temple. They keep the Sabbath, pray in public. These are the main church people. They say, "We have a father. Our father is God."

"No," Jesus says, "you are of your father the devil."

Now I do not care if you are a deacon, I do not care if you are a preacher, if you have not been supernaturally regenerated, if you have not had a miracle we call, and Jesus called "the new birth"; if God has not by His Spirit come in to make you a new man, put in you a heart of flesh instead of that stony heart; then you are a child of the Devil! You are not a child of God. People are not by nature the children of God.

The Lord was good to Mrs. Rice and me. He gave us six wonderful baby girls. What a joy and comfort these girls are to me! They all love the Lord. They all have long hair, and look like Christians. They do not wear pants, do not dress like men. They do not go to movies, nor dance, nor smoke cigarettes. They are happy Christians. They win souls. They sing. They are youthful, godly, good Christian girls, and they are very popular. I thank God for my children. Now let me tell you a sad thing: every one of them was as mean as the Devil when they were born.

You say, "My, but aren't babies beautiful little things?" Yes, they are beautiful.

You say, "Aren't they attractive?" Yes, they are attractive.

You say, "Don't you love them?" Yes, I love them very much, but by nature they are as mean as the Devil. When they are two weeks old, if just you take hold of one and hold his head so he can't look the way he wants to, he will yell bloody murder.

As soon as they are old enough to talk, they lie. When Satan moves one of them, she will reach over and take the other girl's dolly and beat her over the head with it, and run off with it. Children are sinful by nature.

Do not misunderstand me. I did not say they went to Hell or would have gone to Hell had they died when they were babies. I think babies are kept by the grace of God. "As in Adam all die, even so in Christ shall all be made alive." But every last one of them has the taint of sin.

One time Eve held a little baby in her arms, rocked him and said, "I've gotten a man from the Lord." That baby turned out to be a murderer. Every child in this world has the seed of sin and death and Hell in him. Children of the Devil. "Ye are of your father the devil." Children of wrath, children of disobedience, children of this world. That is what the Bible says. Everybody in this world is a child of the Devil until he has a new heart given him by the miracle of God's grace when he is converted, when he is born again. People are not by nature the children of God. They are by nature the children of the Devil, children of wrath, children of this world, children of darkness, the children of disobedience, the Bible says.

4. Born-Again Christians Are Children of God

Here is another blessed truth. Born-again Christians are the children of God. In the first chapter of John, Jesus said,

> "He came unto his own, and his own received him not. But as many as received him, to them gave he power to become the [children of God] sons of God, even to them that believe on his name." John 1:11,12.

Sons of God when you trust Jesus!

> "Which were born, not of blood, nor of the will of the flesh, nor of the will of man, but of God."— John 1:13.

Born of God when you put your trust in Jesus Christ! Again in John, the third chapter, the same thing is taught. Jesus said to Nicodemus.

> "Verily, verily, I say unto thee, Except a man be born again, he cannot see the kingdom of God."— John 3:3.

Then He said,

> "Verily, verily, I say unto thee, Except a man be born of water and of the Spirit, he cannot enter into the kingdom of God."—John 3:5.

And then He said in verse 7,

> "Marvel not that I said unto thee, Ye must be born again."

"Ye must be born again"!

The Bible says, "Beloved, now are we the sons of God, and it doth not yet appear what we shall be." Oh, the wonderful things ahead! I do not know all about them, but, bless God, I know what I am already. I am already a born-again child of God. I am a son of my Father in Heaven. I am a brother of my Elder Brother, Jesus Christ. I am a partaker of the divine nature, the Bible says. The Bible even says that His seed remains in me, so that this new nature, this new-born nature, cannot sin (I John 3:9). Oh, I must struggle as Paul did—"When I would do good, evil was present with me," but I am a child of God.

I am born of God, and so have the blessed Holy Spirit. "Ye have not received the spirit of bondage again to fear; but ye have received the Spirit of adoption, whereby we cry, Abba, Father." Something in my heart makes me not afraid of God. Something in my heart makes me feel I belong to God. He is my father.

I remember some years ago, Dr. Joe Macaulay came to see me at Wheaton. He was then pastor of the Wheaton Bible Church. He came to talk to me about holding revival services in the Wheaton Bible Church. We sat out on the back steps. The young people were playing croquet on the lawn. Joy, my baby girl, was then three years old. She was nearby, and she found a crooked piece of cardboard. I sat on the porch steps, whittling and talking to Dr. Macaulay about this revival. The other folks left us alone. It was a pretty important time. I did not have much time at home, and the good pastor had come to see me. We were planning and praying and talking about the revival, and what we would do about it. My little baby came up with this little bit of a cardboard. She had figured out that one end of it was not square. She held it out there like she wanted it. She held it out to my hands and interrupted our conversation. She said, "Daddy, cut that off." I stopped, took my pocket knife and cut it off so as to make the thing square like she wanted it.

She said, "Thank you, Daddy," and went on about her work. I turned to Brother Macaulay and said, "Any time I want anything, if the Lord God of Heaven and earth is having a conference with all of the archangels, I am going to butt in and say, 'My Father, will You do this for me?' And He will do it!" I have a right to come to my Father. I am born of God, a child of God, inheritor of all the blessings from God.

Over in Galatians, chapter 3, in verse 26,

"For ye are all the children of God by faith in Christ Jesus."

That is the only way anybody gets to be a child of God. You are not a child of God by your natural birth into this world, but a child of God by that second birth—when you put your trust in Jesus. "You are—(all this people here, I am writing to, this church of good Christian people)—Ye are all the children of God by faith in Jesus Christ." In Galatians 4:6,

"And because ye are sons, God hath sent forth the Spirit of his Son into your hearts, crying, Abba, Father."

Ah, I can call God my Father! I saw a woman stand up in prayer meeting and heard her say to the pastor years ago, "I have a neighbor woman who seems very presumptuous to me, brother pastor. She says she knows she is going to Heaven. I don't believe anybody is good enough to know for sure they are going to Heaven." The wise pastor said, "Well, if she is depending on how good she is, it would indeed be presumptuous. But if she is going by the plain Word of God, that she is born again, and if she is going by the fact that God has changed her heart, and her heart says, 'My Father!' and of Heaven, 'my Home, and my destiny,' then she has a right to say 'I am born of God; I am going to Heaven. I know it—because the Bible says so.'"

My Father is rich in houses and lands,
He holdeth the wealth of the world in His hands,
Of rubies and diamonds His coffers are full—

Ah, thank God! I am a child of the King. I am a born-again Christian. It is a wonderful thing to be a child of God. And everybody who has been converted is a child of God. The blessed Holy Spirit comes to live in the heart of a Christian and in the body of a Christian. And his seed remains in the Christian, and the nature of God. We are partakers of the divine nature, Peter says. So, it is a wonderful thing to be born of God. I feel like saying, "My heavenly Father, my Daddy!"

There are some people who say, "I don't think you ought to get too intimate with God." They think we ought to be austere in our approach. They think we ought to be very formal like we were approaching the King of England. But I do not feel that way about my children. Somebody has said to me, "Dr. Rice, I know people who say, 'Dear, dear Jesus. They say, 'Dear, sweet Jesus. They say, 'My precious Saviour. Don't you think that is too intimate? Don't you think that is too personal?" Let me tell you how I feel.

I am pretty hardboiled. Everybody thinks I am a sharp preacher, that I hurt people's feelings, crack down, so they say, "Well his children must all be afraid of him and hate him." No, they do not. They like me very well, and I put up with them pretty good too! We get along very nicely. I like my girls. Yes, sir. When they were little the high chair was always set by my plate, and I fed them. When I came home from meetings, I had good-night prayer with them. It was "Daddy this" and "Daddy that." The first thing everyone of my six daughters learned to say was, "I love Daddy." I just kept working at that, and teaching that.

I used to ride along in the car with my children. When each one was a little bit of a girl, she would stand up in the seat beside me and put her arm around my neck. She would play with my ear or pat me on the head and say, "My sweet Daddy! My sweet Daddy!" Do you think I was insulted? Well, no, I managed to take that very well! Because it was God who put love in her heart for her Daddy. God puts that love in my heart for my heavenly Father. The word, "Abba," is not just the rather austere, formal "My Father"; it is "My Daddy, my Papa," or whatever you call your father, is that familiar and intimate Aramaic word here. "My heavenly Daddy."

Thank God, I am a child of God; and God makes me feel like a child of God. I have the destiny of a child of God, and I am going to be up with God. It is a wonderful thing to be born again.

Let me say another thing about that. I have learned to treasure all the people of God. Somebody said, "Brother Rice, do you know much about this Winebrunner group of the Church of God you are with this week?"

Not too much, but I like them. They love Jesus Christ, believe the Bible, and are under the blood. They say, "I've been saved, brother," and shake my hand. God bless you. I am a Baptist. But I would rather have Christian fellowship with a Catholic priest who can say, "I love Jesus Christ. He is my Saviour. I believe He was born of a virgin. I believe He arose from the dead, after paying for my sins on the cross as my Saviour"—I say I would rather have fellowship with a Catholic priest who can say that, than with a Baptist who is a modernist. I thank God that I can say with the psalmist, "I am a companion of all them that fear thee." I thank God that Jesus said, "Other sheep have I which are not of this fold."

I have preached all over the country, and in Canada. I have preached to immigrants, and I have preached to colored people, etc. Thank God, it just feels the same everywhere, when people know the Lord Jesus. Is not sweet fellowship with born-again Christians wonderful? Yes, I am a brother. If you are born again, then you are my brother.

I brought to this country a colored boy from British Guiana, a little country north of Brazil, in South America.

His name is John Thompson. He talks like an Oxford graduate. His language is very British. I brought him to this country, and, with the help of some friends, put him through Moody Bible Institute. He is doing good work now as assistant pastor of a church in Chicago. To this colored boy, before he came to this country I said, "If you come, you will have to listen to my counsel. I will not be responsible for your schooling unless you treat me as if I were your father and jump when I tell you to jump. I will not bring you over here and let you go your way." He talked it over with his father and his good old Christian father, black as a coal, down in South America, said, "Yes, son. If you go, you must count Dr. Rice your father and ask him about everything." And his good old mother said so, too. (Both his father and his mother have gone to Heaven since John has been in this country.) John Thompson came to this country. He calls me "Father," and he takes very seriously those holy vows. He is thirty years old now. He has been thinking about getting married. Sometime ago he called me on the phone, and wanted to make an appointment so I could meet his girl, a Chicago school teacher, and pass on her.

Some years ago in a Mississippi River flood thousands of colored people were crowded out of their homes in the Louisiana bottom land. They were gathered into large temporary camps and I went and preached among them. Colored people like my preaching because they can understand my language. We had a good time. I preached and they wept and shouted the praises of God. After the service, a good many of them crowded around, colored preachers and others, to shake my hands.

While they were crowded around, one talked to another, and I heard him say, "That man has got a white face, but he sure has got a black heart," by which he meant that I understood and loved colored people, and that I was a brother to those born-again Christians, as I was. A child of God is anyone who is born-again. Anyone who is a child of God is my brother.

II. "The Brotherhood of Man"

Now I must hurry on to the ast part, the brotherhood of man. All saved people are brethren.

1. Saved and Unsaved Are Not Brothers, Spiritually

But not all people in the world

are brothers. Do you think a Christian is a brother to an unsaved man? Turn to II Corinthians, and let us read the Word of God that lives and abides forever.

"Be ye not unequally yoked together with unbelievers." Why not? "For what fellowship hath righteousness with unrighteousness?" Now here is a lost man, unrighteous in his nature. You are a saved man who has the righteousness of God put in his heart, a partaker of the divine nature. "For what fellowship hath righteousness with unrighteousness? and what communion hath light with darkness? And what concord hath Christ with Belial?" (II Cor. 6:14, 15). Here is a saved person—he has Christ in him. Here is a lost person—he has the Devil in him. That is why no Christian ought ever, under any circumstance, marry a lost person. It is a sin. Do not do it. "Or what part hath he that believeth with an infidel?" The word "infidel" here is simply "unbeliever." It does not mean an atheist, but simply one who has not trusted Christ. "And what agreement hath the temple of God with idols? for ye are the temple of the living God." The other man—the Devil lives in him. And in you, if you are a Christian, God lives. If you are a Christian, God is in you. "Ye are the temple of the living God." God has said, "I will dwell in them, and walk in them; and I will be their God, and they shall be my people. Wherefore come out from among them..." (II Cor. 6:17, 18).

You have no business to take unconverted people into the church. You have no business in a lodge, and yoking up with bloody oaths by tying yourself to people who are unconverted. If you are converted you have no business marrying somebody who is unconverted! I am not talking about what church. I am talking about saved and lost. It is light with darkness yoked, which is unequal. It is the Devil and Christ yoked, and that is unequal. That is wrong, the Scripture says.

But it says, 'Come ye out and be ye separate, saith the Lord, and touch not the unclean thing; and I will receive you, And will be a Father unto you, and ye shall be my sons and daughters, saith the Lord Almighty.' (II Cor. 6:17, 18).

Let us see again. Are all people, are lost people and saved people brothers? Are the modernists and the fundamentalists brothers? You people in the denomination—are you to support the missionary program and the colleges and the denominational bosses who do not believe Bible? Are you to put your money in that way? Is your influence to be on that side? Second John, verse 9, 10, and 11.

> "Whosoever transgresseth, and abideth not in the doctrine of Christ, hath not God."—II John **9.**

Someone says, "I don't believe in the virgin birth."

Somebody says, "I don't believe in the inspiration of the Bible."

Somebody said, "I don't believe in the bodily resurrection of Jesus."

Do you know what is wrong with him? "Whosoever transgresseth, and abideth not in the doctrine of Christ [now not incidental doctrines but the doctrines concerning Christ] hath not God." He is not saved. If a man is wrong on the deity of Jesus Christ, the virgin birth, the blood atonement, then he is not a Christian. He does not have God. So what would you do about it? "He that abideth in the doctrine of Christ, he hath both the Father and the Son. If there come any unto you, and bring not this doctrine, receive him not into your house, neither bid him God speed: For he that biddeth him God speed is partaker of his evil deeds" (II John 9-11).

Why are you not to receive him into your house? "Because he is not of God," he is not your brother. He is a child of the Devil. He is going the other way. He is on the other side. He is a different kind of a person. He is darkness. You are light. He is the temple of idols. You are the temple of God. He is the temple of Belial. You are the temple of Christ. So do not have him in your house. Do not say, "God bless you." Do not say, "Here is an offering." Do not say, "Come and eat dinner with me." You just pray for him like any other old sinner.

Are all the people in the world brothers? No. A lawyer called me on the telephone when I was pastor at Dallas and said, "Dr. Rice, I just can't believe that God would send one of His children to Hell. Why, I wouldn't send one of my children to Hell, no matter what he did."

I said, "God doesn't send His children to Hell either. It's just the Devil's children that God sends to Hell. Why should God look after the Devil's children."

You look to your own Daddy. The Devil's children go to their own Hell. They made the way for it. "The wages of sin is death." That is where they belong. They have no claim on God. They are not children of God. They would not let God make them sons. They would not let God change their hearts. They would not let God change their natures. They are children of wrath—and that is their choice.

Only those who have been born again are brothers. Should we love people? Yes, love sinners everywhere; weep over them, pray for them, preach to them. But do not call them your brothers, do not count them spiritually your brothers, do not yoke up with them, do not support them in their false doctrines.

2. Christians Are Brothers of the Lord Jesus

Now let us see then another verse. Did you know we are brothers of the Lord Jesus? What a wonderful truth this is! Brothers of the Lord Jesus! The Scripture says very plainly in Hebrews 2, verses 10, 11, and 12.

"For it became him, for whom are all things, and by whom are all things,"

that is, God provided everything for Him, and He turned all creation over to Jesus Christ.

"For whom are all things, and by whom are all things, in bringing many sons unto glory, to make the captain of their salvation perfect through sufferings. For both he that sanctifieth and they who are sanctified are all of one: for which cause he is not ashamed to call them brethren."

The Lord, by His death on the cross, paid our debts, set us apart for God for ever. That means he sanctified us. But the one who does the sanctifying, and the one who gets sanctified are one. "And he is not ashamed to call us brethren," the Scripture says, "Saying, I will declare thy name unto my brethren, in the midst of the church will I sing praise unto thee." We are going to have a wonderful song up in Heaven. Jesus Christ will sing a solo part of it. He is going to sing it with His brethren in the church. He is going to call all of us His brethren. Jesus Christ, my older Brother. Jesus Christ, my Brother, and yours, if you are a child of God. In verse 17, "Wherefore in all things it behoved him to be made like unto his brethren. . ."

Jesus says, "John Rice was born in this world. I will be born down there, too."

Jesus said, "John Rice is very poor sometimes. I am going to be poor, too."

Jesus said, "John Rice will be tempted. All right, I will let the old Devil do his worst on me, too, and tempt me, and I will whip him. Then John Rice is going to have to have some way to lick the Devil. Well, I will show him how to do it with the Word of God and the power of the Holy Spirit."

"And all may be made like I am —born of a woman, nursed at a mother's breast, lived in poverty, suffered all temptations." He was weary as I have been weary. He was tossed and hated and despised, as sometimes men are hated and despised. He died and we have to die, too. Thank God, we can come boldly. "We have not a high priest who cannot be touched with the feelings of our infirmities, but one who was in all points tempted like as we are, yet without sin" (Heb. 4:15). Oh, such a Saviour! Such a brother! Such an Elder Brother, our Saviour! Is not that wonderful news?

3. We Should Feel Responsible to Win Our Blood Brothers

Now I come to the last word. We have our own blood brothers. I wonder how many have unsaved brothers? What a comfort it is to me that all my five brothers and my three sisters are saved. As far as I know, the nieces and nephews are all saved. My little granddaughter, only six years old, on her sixth birthday came to Jesus. I surely would not sleep well tonight if I thought some intimate relative, somebody near and dear, was unsaved.

I have two younger preacher brothers. I went down to Baylor University. We did not have any money. I said to my brother, "George, come on down here. I will let you sleep with me in my little attic room. (I paid $4 a month for it.) I will help you get a job here at the University. You can room with me." And I said,

"George, I've got a girl picked out for you, a fine Christian girl." He came down and lived with me in my little attic room and went to the University. I helped get him jobs. He started out to make good, and went on and finished. And he married the girl I had picked out for him. A fellow owes something to his brother.

Bill and Joe came on—both of them are preachers, and I believe that on the human side it is largely because I was a preacher, and because they had heard me preach, and because they laid everything on the altar under my preaching. Oh, what will you do if you have loved ones unsaved and going to Hell! Blood ties ought to be very close. The man in Hell could not rest in Hell, tormented in flames. He could not rest thinking about his five brothers. He said, "I have five brothers back in my father's house. I was the older brother. I made lots of money. I gave a big banquet. I had lots of drinking, had all the wild parties. I made the money and had the big times, clothed in purple and fine linen. And my younger brothers all started out to do just like their big brother, all trying to make money and all trying to spend it for pleasures of the flesh." He said, "Send Lazarus back to preach to my brothers before they come to this place of torment." Down in Hell a man remembered his brothers. Is it not strange that in Lancaster County, Pennsylvania, some of you have unconverted loved ones, but you never lift a finger to win your own brother, to win your own sister, to win your own boy or girl? Is not that sad, and strange? What a commentary on the coldness of your faith and of your love to Christ when you do not take the Gospel to your own! Ah, blood brothers are so near. Let us win them while we can. I hope you will.

I had the joy of winning my brother Joe's wife just before they were married. I won some of my own children, Mrs. Rice won some of them. Oh, win your own loved ones while you can.

Lost man, do you want to be a child of God? Would it not be wonderful if God would come in and give you a new heart and make you a child of God, and put the new nature inside? Would it not be wonderful if Jesus said, "I am going to be an older Brother to this boy, this girl, this man, this woman. I will be Saviour. I will be King. I will be Preacher. I will be Friend. But most of all, I will be a Brother, beside him all the time, an Elder Brother"? Do you not want Jesus?

You say, "Could I have God as my Father?"

Yes.

"Could I feel free to come and call God, Father, and tell him all my burdens and thank Him for salvation, and know I am a child of God and know I am going to Heaven?"

Yes, thank God, you can. You can do it tonight, and go home saved and happy. How is that? Here it is: "You are all the children of God, by faith in Jesus Christ." When you put your trust in Jesus, "To as many as received him, to them gave he power to become the sons of God, even to them that believe on his name." (John 1:12) Do you want to be saved tonight?

I am not talking about what church you join; I am talking about Jesus. I am not talking about reforming; I am talking about your being re-born. I am not talking about turning over a new leaf; I am talking about God giving you a new heart. Do you want a new heart today?

My friend Fred Hawkins who owns the Fred Hawkins Mills down in Springfield, Missouri, was converted twelve years ago. He had been a member of the church many years. He was a cussing, whiskey-drinking, unconverted church member. A man came to talk to him about his soul almost every day for three months except Sunday. The occasion he had for talking to him was that he bought feed for his dairy cattle from this feed mill. Fred said, "That man bought so much goods from me, I didn't want to make him mad. So I listened to him every day." The dairyman would never buy enough feed for his cattle for a week, but just enough for one day, then he would come back the next day and bring his Bible and talk to Fred about his soul and buy enough feed for one day. Then on Saturday enough for two days, then Monday back again with his Bible. He kept that up for three months.

Then Fred Hawkins got so convicted, finally he went down in the basement of his mill early one morning at five o'clock. He said, "I didn't want anybody to see me." (Imagine somebody looking through the window at five o'clock in the morning!) He went down to the basement and kneeled down on the floor there, and said, "Lord, I won't promise you a thing. I won't promise you I'll quit drinking. I promised my wife that and never could. I won't promise you I'll quit smoking. I won't promise you I'll quit my cussing. I cuss even before women. I am so embarrassed about it. I've promised, and I can't do it. I won't promise you anything, Lord. But my friend keeps telling me that You give fellows new hearts. If You've got a new heart, I wish You would give me one. I sure need a new one. This old mean wicked heart has gone so far in sin. If you would give me a new heart, I wish you would." He got up from there and went on his way.

A day or two later, he dropped something on his finger and crushed it and had to go to the doctor. It was very painful. The doctor put some medicine on it and dressed it. Then he got to thinking, "That's funny. I didn't cuss. What do you know about that? That's the first thing that ever happened to me that I didn't cuss about. Come to think of it, I haven't cussed for three days!" God gave him a new heart. He said, "I haven't cussed since. Didn't want to." He drove me down through southern Missouri, and he said, "That Honky Tonk there I used to drink there." Then again, "I used to get drunk with the boys over here." He drove down the road and he turned to me, tears running down his face, and he said, "Brother John, I just thank

God I don't want it any more. I just thank God I'm not interested. I have something so much better." Born-again, a new heart, a child of God! You see? God help you.

Do you want to be a child of God? Do you want to be born of God so you can say, "God is my Father and Christians are my brethren. Jesus is my Saviour, my Elder Brother. I'm headed for Heaven"? Oh, the inheritance prepared of God for His sons! Do you want that? You can have it if you will turn to Christ.

The Double Curse of Booze

"Woe to the crown of pride, to the drunkards of Ephraim, whose glorious beauty is a fading flower, which are on the head of the fat valleys of them that are overcome with wine!"—Isa. 28:1.

"The crown of pride, the drunkards of Ephraim, shall be trodden under feet."—Isa. 28:3.

"But they also have erred through wine, and through strong drink are out of the way; the priest and the prophet have erred through strong drink, they are swallowed up of wine, they are out of the way through strong drink; they err in vision, they stumble in judgment. For all tables are full of vomit and filthiness, so that there is no place clean."—Isa. 28:7, 8.

"Woe unto him that giveth his neighbour drink, that puttest thy bottle to him, and makest him drunken also, that thou mayest look on their nakedness! Thou art filled with shame for glory; drink thou also, and let thy foreskin be uncovered: the cup of the Lord's right hand shall be turned unto thee, and shameful spewing shall be on thy glory."—Hab. 2:15, 16.

Notice the woe to the crown of pride, the drunkards of Ephraim. Woe to the drunkard! A curse is on the drunkard, says the Word of God. There is a curse on the man who drinks, on the woman who drinks.

There is another curse: "Woe unto him that giveth his neighbour drink, that puttest thy bottle to him, and makest him drunken also, that thou mayest look on their nakedness!" There is a curse on the person who serves, who sells, who gives liquor.

By way of introduction, let me say this: in Bible times they did not have distilled whisky as we have it now. However, they did have several kinds of wine. But wine in the New Testament very often means simply grapejuice. In fact, there was not in Bible times a different word for wine and for grapejuice as we have. When the juice was first squeezed out of the grapes, it was called *wine,* as you see from Proverbs 3:10: "So shall thy barns be filled with plenty, and thy presses shall burst out with new wine." So grapejuice is wine, in the Bible sense. Later when the grapejuice ferments, it is still wine in the Bible sense.

There is no reason to suppose that the wine which Jesus made at the wedding in John, chapter 2, was intoxicating wine. There is no reason to suppose that that which was used at the last supper and which New Testament churches used for the Lord's Supper was intoxicating wine. In fact, the Scripture takes particular pains not to call it wine, but instead calls it "the cup," and "the fruit of the vine." So the Lord seems to have specially guarded against being misunderstood on this point. However, if He had used the word *wine* it might have meant unfermented wine, that is, simply grapejuice.

I. God's Curse on Drinkers

Tonight I call your attention to the double curse of God on booze.

First, there is a curse on the drunkard. Who is a drunkard? When is a man drunk? Many a man, after he has been arrested for killing somebody with his car, or after a fatal accident, says to the judge, "Why, Judge, I only had two or three beers. I wasn't drunk." He couldn't drive well, couldn't see well. He couldn't get his foot on the brake as quickly as he ought to; he was not as reliable a driver under the influence of liquor. But he said he wasn't drunk. Because he wasn't unconscious or wasn't in a stupor, he thinks he wasn't drunk.

When is a man drunk? When a man has drunk, he is drunk. Anybody who drinks beverage alcohol in any degree is somewhat affected by it, and so he is drunk to that degree. A man can get more drunk than he already is. He can drink until he is drunk, then he can drink until he is more drunk, then he can drink until he is unconscious and can't drink any more. A man can drink until a certain percentage of alcohol gets into the blood and stops the motor responses so that he quits breathing and dies. Now, that is a little more drunk than he was while he was breathing. Yet he is still drunk.

There is no way one can make a law and say when a man has passed a certain point, then he is drunk. Any man who drinks alcohol has some alcohol content in the blood that affects his nerve reaction, his muscular co-ordination, his mind, his disposition. And so the man is in some measure drunk.

You know that the word *drunk* is part of the verb *to drink* drink, drank, drunk; or, drink, drank, drunken. A drunkard is a man who drinks. Anybody who drinks any alcoholic liquor is under the influence of it, is affected by it, and to that degree is drunk.

If it takes eight glasses of beer to make a man drunk (it takes less than that for some people) then the man who has one glass is one-eighth drunk. The man who has two glasses is one-fourth drunk. And no man one-fourth drunk is safe as an engineer of a passenger train, safe to drive an automobile down the road, or safe to handle a steam shovel, or a drill press, or a welding torch. No girl who is one-fourth drunk is safe in the presence of sex temptation. The man who would not gamble without drinking, will gamble when he is one-fourth drunk. And the man who never intended to take more than two glasses of beer can be tempted to take more when he is already one-fourth drunk!

You see, one lie is not as bad as eight lies, but it is still a lie! And a man with one glass of beer in his system may not be in as great a danger as the man with eight glasses of beer in his system, but he is still drunk enough to kill somebody with his car, drunk enough to say things he would not say if he were sober, drunk enough to make the wrong decisions, drunk enough to take another drink if the temptation comes strongly. What would sound profane a few minutes ago now sounds funny. The suggestion that was indecent sometime ago now seems, to the brain which is beginning to be stupefied by a very small amount of alcohol, to be very reasonable.

The man who drinks would commit adultery under the influence of liquor when he would not commit the same sin sober. The girl who drinks will permit familiarites and enter into sin that would make her shudder if she were sober. The higher brain centers that control moral sense and responsibility are deadened first by alcohol.

Then muscular control begins to slacken. A man cannot see accurately. Tests show that a man with two glasses of beer is not nearly as good a marksman with a rifle as before he drank. The man with two or three glasses of beer in his stomach begins to be a very unsafe driver. He may feel that he drives better, but actually he drives much worse. He has no sense of danger, no sense of moral responsibility, but his foot is slower on the pedal and his hand is slower on the steering wheel.

The truth is, the first glass of liquor has the same kind of alcohol that the eighth glass has.

Somebody remarks, "But, Brother Rice, it is only 3.2 beer." Well, don't take that too seriously. Anybody who makes beer is a lawbreaker. One who doesn't mind breaking hearts, and breaking homes, and making paupers and harlots and drunkards and damning souls, wouldn't mind breaking the law. The whisky business, the beer business, the wine business has down through the years been run by lawbreakers who would bribe legislators, who would sell to minors against the law, who would be open at illegal hours, who would do anything to make more money. Don't trust the conscience nor the good citizenship of any one who is in the business of making drunkards. He doesn't have much of a conscience, for he would do most anything for money.

So don't put too much stock in the fact that it is just 3.2 beer you have down here in West Virginia. Many a man, if he can, gets by by making it five per cent or six per cent, if he can sell more of it. A man who would sell 3.2 beer to damn souls, would sell six per cent beer to damn more souls, if he could get more money out of it. So don't ever trust anybody who is in the business of making money out of human misery.

When a man drinks beer, he learns to want the alcohol in liquor, or more effect, as he says; so he drinks whisky or rum or something else that has more alcohol to it than does beer. It is not whether you call it beer, whether you call it wine, whether you call it whisky. Beverage alcohol is a hateful, wicked thing with the curse of God on it because it makes drunkards and brings all the train of evils that go with it.

The Woe of Poverty Caused By Drink

Now what are some of the curses of God on the drunkard? Listen to Proverbs 23:21:

"For the drunkard and the glutton shall come to poverty: and drowsiness shall clothe a man with rags."

What is the curse on the drunkard? Poverty. I need not prove that. How many of you here ever knew somebody who was poor because of liquor?

In the second grade at school I had my first love affair! I fell in love with Miss Mabel Blossom, my second grade teacher! One day Miss Mabel said to the class, "All you children but Sammy will have to stay in today. Sammy, you have been a good boy. You may go home on time. Get your lunch bucket, your cap and coat, and go on home. Good-by, Sammy. I am going to keep the rest of the class in."

Sammy left. When the door was closed, Miss Mabel got off her rostrum, walked down near us, stood there with tears in her eyes as she said, "Children, some of you haven't been very nice to Sammy. You don't like to play with him. You have nice lunch baskets, while he brings his lunch—if he has anything at all—in a lard pail. Your Mother fixes your hair nice. You little girls have nice starched dresses; you little boys have white blouses and clean pants, but little Sammy only wears dirty old patched overalls." She said, "Children, I want to tell you something. Sammy is not to blame. His father is a drunkard, and Sammy's mother does the best she can. They don't have money a lot of the time. Sammy can't bring any lunch some days. So don't you be mean to Sammy. He can't help it if his father drinks."

I have never gotten away from that. Here is a little boy who didn't have lunches like the rest of us. Our family was very poor, but we always had clothes enough, and they were always clean. We came with our hair combed and looked nice. We were well cared for. But Sammy, with a drinking father, couldn't have nice clothes; he didn't have enough to eat, and he went barefoot in the wintertime. I was impressed then with the thing I have wept over I guess a thousand times since—the poverty of wives and little children who suffer because of a husband or daddy who is a drunkard.

Many of you have known such

cases. Sometimes the wife took in washing or did other hard work to try to make a living because the husband and father was a drunkard.

Once while I was preaching in a certain city, I believe in North Carolina, a preacher friend pointed out to me a certain man, now an old bum. There was a stubble of beard on his face unshaven; his clothes were dirty and unpressed; his hair long; his eyes bloodshot. He had on a dirty old slouch hat. "Do you have any idea who that man is?" he asked me. Of course I didn't know. "That is Senator So and So who used to represent this state in the United States Senate. But drink brought him down. It made him lose votes; he couldn't attend to his business, then when he tried to run his law office, he couldn't get clients. Now he is just an old drunken bum."

You would be surprised to find if you had been where I have been —in the Evansville Rescue Mission, in the Pacific Garden Mission in Chicago, in the Bowery Mission in New York City, in the Mel Trotter Mission in Grand Rapids—how many university graduates, how many business executives, how many lawyers and doctors and men of good position have, because of drink, come to want and to where they couldn't hold a job, couldn't take care of their families and who came to abject poverty, came to picking up cigarette butts off the streets and knocking at back doors for a handout. Yes, "the drunkard and the glutton shall come to poverty."

Years ago in Decatur, Texas, I held a revival campaign. My father, in a Chevrolet car, hooked on to the block and tackle and pulled up the eight-hundred-pound tent center poles. Some men helped me drive the stakes; we put up the big tent and held a revival.

On one corner of the same block was a garage. In that garage lived a drunkard with his family. Though it was during prohibition days, yet he was a drunkard. One day as I went into the back of that garage, I saw some bed springs, not a mattress, just the springs with a couple of quilts on them. That was the sleeping place of the two boys of the family. The only wall or partition was a sheet which was hung on a string. This cut off that greasy, dirty part of the floor of the garage from the public workshop. That was the only home for that family of four. Each of the children had only one pair of faded, dirty, dingy blue overalls. His wife had no change of clothing. They were in the barest scrapings of poverty.

The man, this drunken man, was a good mechanic. He sold lots of gasoline through his fuel pumps. But he never stayed sober long enough to make a good living. Nearly everything he had went for liquor.

Once during the revival campaign that man stood against the corner of the garage and heard me preach. I prayed for God to reach his heart. The next night he again stood there and listened. The third night Dad persuaded him to come over and stand by the corner of the tent. He had no clothes but overalls, so he would not come into the tent. That night at the invitation, my father, with his arms around him, led him to Christ. He was wonderfully saved.

Isn't it wonderful what God can do for a drunkard? Isn't it wonderful what He can do for a sinner?

Then the man buckled down to work. I went by to see him. When people found he was sober, they began to bring their cars to him, for he was a genuine mechanic. He could fix anything. He had plenty of work.

One day a truck backed up to that old garage and a Singer sewing machine was unloaded. The woman began making clothes. A few days later she came to me and said, "Brother Rice, we've rented a three-room house! It has a sink, running water and electric lights, and gas to cook with. We are moving there tomorrow."

The next day the moving truck loaded the little trinkets. A pickup truck could haul all they had. They put in the sewing machine, the bed springs, a few old quilts, and a broken-down chair or two, took them over to the house, and they started housekeeping.

Yes, poverty, trouble, broken homes, pale-faced widows and little children without shoes in the winter are a natural picture of what inevitably comes when people go on in drink. Broken homes, broken hearts are the results of drink. The roses leave the bride's cheeks. With a broken heart she holds on as long as she can. Cold houses, ill-clad children, curses and beating, no money with which to buy food, are her lot. After awhile she gives up. Then other women come in. A man who drinks has no sense, no loyalty, no character. Everything is gone. Oh, the curse of God is on liquor.

The way drunkenness brings poverty and a ruined home and life is well expressed by Talmage:

It takes everything that is sacred in the family, everything that is holy in religion, everything that is infinite in the soul, and tramples it into the mire.

The marriage day has come. The happy pair at the altar. The music sounds. The gay lights flash. The feet bound up and down the drawing room. Started on a bright voyage of life. Sails all up. The wind is abaft. You prophesy everything beautiful.

But the scene changes. A dingy garret. No fire. On a broken chair sits a sorrowing woman. Her last hope gone. Poor, disgraced, trodden underfoot— she knows the despair of being a drunkard's wife. The gay barque that danced off on the marriage morning has become a battered hulk, dismasted and shipwrecked. "Oh," she says, "he was as good a man as ever lived. He was so kind, so generous— no one better did God ever create than he; but the drink! The drink did it!"

Listen, the girl who marries a man who drinks is looking for poverty and heartbreak, and she will get it. The Scripture makes it clear there will be quarrels and trouble for the man who drinks. You know that. Oh, little children born in a drunkard's home are cursed before they are born. Poverty is the curse of a drinker.

The Curse of Contention, Quarrels, Goes With Drink

Let me read again in Proverbs 23, beginning with verse 29:

"Who hath woe? who hath sorrow? who hath contentions? [You know who has contentions, don't you? In the home where there has been drinking.] *who has babbling?* [silly talk] *who hath wounds without cause?* [got into a fight] *who hath redness of eyes? They that tarry long at the wine; they that go to seek mixed wine. Look not thou upon the wine when it is red, when it giveth his colour in the cup, when it moveth itself aright. At the last it biteth like a serpent, and stingeth like an adder."*

Who is it that hath contentions, woe, babbling? Who hath wounds without cause? They that tarry at the wine.

What a fascination there is about alcoholic drink! The sense of luxury, of expensive, bubbling champagne! The hilarity of the cocktail party! The pleasant warmth of the toddy, the stimulation of brandy, the convivial sociability of beer!

Fortified by liquor, the timid man becomes bold. The wallflower becomes, she thinks, the wittiest conversationalist! After a few drinks, every joke is funny, every remark is brilliant, the casual stranger becomes a bosom friend. Sorrows are forgotten for the moment. Conscience troubles no more. Marriage ties, holy vows, honest responsibilities—these all lose their hold under the influence of drink. So one seems to be more carefree. People seem friendlier, life seems gayer. Satan offers many attractions in alcoholic drink.

In Winston-Salem, North Carolina, one night my daughter Grace, Miss Viola and I went for a snack after the service. As we started back to the hotel two drunks came alongside us. One came up close—he wanted to talk. I said, "Now get away; don't bother us." But he put his hand on my shoulder, then I said, "If you don't take your hand off, I'll knock you down. I will not put up with it."

Many a man gets his face bashed in when he is drinking because he can't behave. Nobody is safe company who drinks. A drunkard hasn't any sense about treating people right and keeping the peace. How can a man expect a wife to live with him in peace? You can put it down that drink brings wounds without cause, brings contentions and quarrels. Drink brings broken homes. How many divorces are brought about by booze! That is part of the curse God has put on the drunkard. "Woe to the drunkard," the Bible says.

And I want to lay on your hearts how wicked it is to expect to do a decent day's work or to bear any responsibility when you have already sold out part of your brain. I say, a man doesn't have control of himself.

The Curse of Deadened Moral Sensibilities

And then the curse on the drinker is that the man's eyes and brain are deadened first. Somebody may say, "Alcohol is a stimulant." No, primarily alcohol is a narcotic. That is the reason after awhile a man goes to sleep if he drinks. It tends to dull the nerves. It tends to dull the sensibility. Alcohol first stupefies the higher brain centers.

In Gainesville, Texas, where I lived when I was a boy, people would sometimes get drunk, then go out to the sidewalk and say, "If I can walk this line in the sidewalk, I'm not too drunk to go home." If they could walk that line, they were still all right.

But long before that a man is drunk at the top end. Long before he cannot walk a line he is unfit to run a bus, unfit to be a railroad engineer, unfit to drive a plane, unfit to drive on the highway, unfit to take a girl to the movies, unfit to date a decent woman, because the man part is now stupified and drunk. The beast part is still there; the animal part can still walk and use his hands. A man is pretty far gone even before he cannot see straight, pretty far gone before he cannot hold a cup of water without spilling it. Liquor attacks the top part first.

Now the truth is though you may still be able to stand on your legs, your brain has been cooked pretty well with alcohol. This is the principle on which all medicine is used. There is one kind of chemical, one kind of drug that will go to one part of the body, and have an effect there while another kind of chemical or drug will go to another part of the body and have an effect there. For example, some drugs will affect the liver. Other drugs will affect the heart such as digitalis, or nitroglycerin tablets. Some drugs will stimulate the gastric juices.

Now there are several kinds of alcohol. Wood alcohol goes immediately to the optic nerves. And many people are temporarily if not permanently blinded from drinking wood alcohol. Rubbing alcohol is poisonous and so sometimes kills people. Each kind of alcohol has an affinity for certain parts of the body.

The alcohol in beer, whisky and wine, which is sometimes grain alcohol, soaks into the brain and some of it is actually absorbed into the brain. It goes first into the blood, and of course is carried to the brain. In the highest centers of control, I mean where conscience is, one is drunk first. The brain relaxes control in the area of moral inhibitions. I mean the part that inhibits and says, "Go easy. Remember you are your mother's boy. Remember your reputation." The part that says to a woman, "Remember, you are a wife and mother," or to a nice sweet girl, "Remember, you are a pure girl"—that part dies first. It takes but a few spoonfuls of alcohol to deaden that part.

Now what do you have? Give a woman who is quiet and modest just one or two drinks and now she is loud-talking, laughing at her own jokes, patting everybody on the back. Now she is not careful to arrange her skirt, not concerned if her hair is ruffled and unkempt. I am just saying that it is a terrible curse of liquor at the top part, the brain, the finer instincts. The civilized person, the cultured person, the person who takes responsibility is the part that gets drunk first. The higher centers of the brain become anesthetized, become narcotized first and so one can't control himself. Alcohol goes first to the higher centers of the brain and then to certain areas that control sex functions so then a man's sex desires increase, but his control, the thing that makes him talk softly and like a gentleman, is gone. Now he will talk loud and coarse and vulgar and swear and insult women. He can still walk straight. He can still drive his car, but the gentleman part gets drunk before the rest of him does. What is left is the brute part. But the brain part, the gentleman part, is the first part that gets drunk. I want you to remember that. That part that tells the truth is affected first by alcohol. The higher quality of mind and character first gets drunk.

I warn you now: as certain as there is a God in Heaven, when you take liquor in your mouth, you risk everything sacred, everything pure, everything holy, everything valuable! A curse of God is on the one who drinks.

Liquor and Lewdness, Drink and Adultery

Another curse of liquor is a curse of sex desire. It is many times mentioned in the Bible. Let me read it again here in Habakkuk 2:15, 16:

"Woe unto him that giveth his neighbour drink, that puttest thy bottle to him, and makest him drunken also, that thou mayest look on their nakedness! Thou art filled with shame for glory: drink thou also, and let thy foreskin be uncovered: the cup of the Lord's right hand shall be turned unto thee, and shameful spewing shall be on thy glory."

Evidently it was known in Bible times that drunkenness made people take off their clothes and be immoral. There was Noah, a good man. God said that he, his wife, his three sons and their wives, were the only ones of his entire generation worth saving. So God killed the whole race except them. Noah was a good man, one who walked with God. God spared him. But after he got out of the ark he planted a vineyard and then he made wine and got drunk. Do not say that he was intentionally bad, for he was not. But Noah got drunk. And the Bible tells in Genesis, chapter 9, how he lay naked in his tent. There, drunk and naked, his boy looked on him and laughed and laughed. Others, ashamed, came and covered their drunken dad, lying naked in the tent and not caring. That is what happens when people drink.

Turn to the nineteenth chapter of Genesis and we have the story of Lot. The wicked city of Sodom was destroyed and Lot and his two daughters were taken out of the city and dwelt in a cave in the mountains. Lot had wine in the cave. And his two daughters talked among themselves and said, "It looks as if all the men in the world are killed, all the boys we knew, and we are going to turn out to be old maids, and not have a family. So let's make Dad drunk." And they got the old man to drink wine and then, under the influence of the wine, they each lay with their father and conceived through this wicked incest. And both of them became unmarried mothers.

That tragic story is an eternal indictment against liquor. Don't tell me that wine is better than whisky, when wine is the kind of drink that will make a man like Lot so that he hasn't any sensibility, so his conscience is seared, so the sense of his own decency is gone. Now, drunken and committing incest with his own daughters. Liquor does that!

Now what part of a man gets drunk first? The pilot, that part that is the control; the part that holds the reins, that guides the steering, that controls the passions and keeps a man or woman straight. I say, drunkenness leads to adultery, leads to nakedness, leads to lewdness.

In Exodus is the story of the Ten Commandments, given by God to Moses upon Mount Sinai. When Moses and Joshua came down off the mountain they heard music and shouting. When they got down they found the people had said to Aaron, "Make us gods to worship," and gave him earrings and bracelets. So Aaron molded a golden calf and they worshipped it. Exodus 32:6 says:

"And they rose up early on the morrow, and offered burnt-offerings, and brought peace-offerings: and the people sat down to eat and drink, and rose up to play."

After they drank, what happened? God's Word tells us in Exodus 32:25:

"And when Moses saw that the people were naked; (for Aaron had made them naked unto their shame among their enemies....)"

Now why is it when people drink that they do not mind pulling off their clothes? Do not mind cursing and blaspheming? Why is it when people drink they have no respect for God, no respect for womanhood, no care about little children? When a man drinks, why is it that he does not care whether his children have food or not? When a woman drinks, why is it that she does not mind leaving her babies shut up in a cold house while she goes to a tavern and spends the night drinking with soldiers and others? There is something horrible in the drink that steals away the brain, steals away the conscience, takes away modesty, takes away holy impulses in the mind and heart!

Listen, I care not whether you are the best man or woman in the world, the most respected, how much you love God, how virtuous your mind, how true your conscience; you take a few drinks and that sense is gone. One cannot be trusted who drinks. You cannot be trusted to drive a car. You cannot be trusted with another man's wife. You cannot be trusted to pay your honest debts. You cannot be trusted to take care of your children.

It does not take eight glasses of beer to make you drunk. When you drink the first glass, you are one-eighth drunk. And that first glass goes to your head. The last glass may make you so your legs will wobble. The last glass may make you so you will go to sleep in a drunken stupor. But the first glass is the part that destroys the fine appreciation, the inhibition that keeps you from doing wrong, the sense of responsibility that makes you bring home your pay check, makes you take care of your children. That part that makes you respect virtue, that makes you tell the truth, makes you keep out of crime—that part is dead first, doped first, cursed first. God said, "Woe to the crown of pride, to the drunkards of Ephraim." Woe to the drunkard! What a curse on drink!

Now what I am saying is that liquor stirs sex appetite and leads people to do what they would not otherwise do. That is why bawdy houses used to be in the second story above saloons. And that is why liquor and immorality go regularly together now. There is much more like that in the Bible.

In Proverbs, chapter 23, the Scripture says:

"Look not thou upon the wine when it is red . . . . Thine eyes shall behold strange women [foreign women or harlot women, not your own wife, so therefore strange to you], *and thine heart shall utter perverse things. Yea, thou shalt be as he that lieth down in the midst of the sea, or as he that lieth upon the top of a mast. They have stricken me, shalt thou say, and I was not sick; they have beaten me, and I felt it not: when shall I awake? I will seek it yet again."*

A man who was loyal to his wife, now becomes a whoremonger. A man who was decent in his language, now when he drinks a little, is profane and lewd. Why? The higher centers are affected first with liquor, and the man who was moral becomes immoral. Sex passion is stirred by alcohol. The man who was first a decent man becomes of unusual sex passion and desire, and is led into sin. "Thine eyes shall behold strange women." It will be with you as it was with Lot and with many others.

What is the curse on the drunkard? "Woe to the crown of pride, to the drunkards of Ephraim." What is the curse besides poverty, besides quarrels and trouble and broken homes?

The Drinker Is Enslaved By Drink

A man then becomes a slave to drink. One of the most pitiful things is that a man who drinks and drinks cannot quit. Somebody will be like that drunken barber in Chicago. His wife stayed with him though she went through hell on earth because her husband couldn't pass drink by. He would promise her that he would quit, but he couldn't quit. The next day he would be dead drunk.

One day their little girl fell sick and the anxious wife pleaded, "Call the doctor." They called the doctor and he informed them that the little one must have medicine right away, and he wrote out a prescription. The wife asked the husband to get the medicine and to come right back. She had saved up some money. "If I give you the money, will you get the medicine and hurry back?" "Yes," he said. So she gave him the prescription and money. He went down towards the drugstore, but on the way he passed a saloon. His appetite overpowered him so that he didn't get back for more than a day. The money was spent on drink. When he did come back the little girl had died, and was in the coffin.

Of course he was brokenhearted. His grief was overwhelming. He stood in the front room by that little casket, looked on his little darling—dead because he didn't get back with the medicine—and wept. But even beside her coffin he became thirsty for drink. "Oh, this sorrow! If I could drown it in drink, I wouldn't be so miserable!" he reasoned with himself. Some neighbors had bought the baby some pretty little red shoes and dressed her for the funeral. He saw those little shoes on his precious baby, then slipped them off, put them in his pocket, went down to the bartender and traded them for a drink!

A man becomes enslaved. One such man said to me, "Brother Rice, there is no use of my making any promises. Before my wife and mother I opened a vein, took a pen and dipped it in the blood and signed a pledge in my own blood and swore I would never taste liquor again. But in twenty-four hours I was drunk."

In Amarillo, Texas, I preached one night to a great crowd in a tabernacle. After the service four of us preachers went back to the Capitol Hotel to talk and pray. The phone rang. A man's voice said, "I want somebody to talk and pray for me. I am a poor sinner who needs help." We told him to come on down to our room. He came and said, "Gentlemen, I am not dressed. I am drunk, but I need God. I sure wish somebody would pray for me." We tried to show this twenty-six-year-old man how to be saved from the Scriptures. Then we knelt together and prayed.

I prayed, another preacher prayed, this man prayed. Oh, what a brokenhearted prayer! He pleaded, "O God, I want to be a good boy like my mother wanted me to be. Lord, you know last year I made $26,000 selling life insurance. I cheated the government out of income tax on half of it. O God, I have been awfully sinful. But won't You forgive me?" He had tried to commit suicide by jumping out of a third-story window. His wife had left him because he couldn't let liquor alone. He had spent weeks in a hospital; now he was down here to pray. We asked God to save him and I believe God did.

Then after he had trusted Christ as Saviour, one of the preachers said to him, "I would make up my mind with all the willpower of my soul that I would never touch liquor again at any cost."

That man looked at us with the most pitiful look and said, "I don't have any willpower anymore! I once did, but I don't now. It will take something besides willpower." Thank God for a Christ who can fix a fellow who can't fix himself!

Yes, one becomes a slave to

drink. I saw a man in his own home, with his wife beside him weeping—I saw that man put his head in his hands, shake it and say, "Brother Rice, my wife doesn't believe it. She thinks I don't care. She thinks I don't love God, nor her, nor the boys. But oh, if I could just get hold of myself! I wish I would never taste it again. I don't want to." Many a man is enslaved by drink.

But I bring you good news. Bless God, the Lord Jesus came to set the captive free. He came to fix the man who can't fix himself.

How many times I have seen Him put a home back together, put a man back in his job, make it so a man can make a living again for his children. I have seen God make it so a man could have control of himself again. But the terrible thing is that it makes a slave out of a man so that he can't leave it alone. That is part of the curse of the drunkard. "Woe to the crown of pride, to the drunkards of Ephraim." Woe to the drunkard. The curses on the drunkard!

The Woe of Hell for Drunkards

Then there is another thing— the worst curse of all on the drunkard. I read to you from I Corinthians 6:9 and 10:

"Know ye not that the unrighteous shall not inherit the kingdom of God? Be not deceived: neither fornicators, nor idolaters, nor adulterers, nor effeminate, nor abusers of themselves with mankind, Nor thieves, nor covetous, nor drunkards, nor revilers, nor extortioners, shall inherit the kingdom of God."

"Drunkards . . . shall not inherit the kingdom of God."

My friend, that is a terrible curse. A drunkard's home is a place where there probably are no carpets on the floor. It may be a home that is a hell on earth. It may be a home where children hide when Dad comes in at night. It may be a place where the roses leave the bride's cheek and love flies out the window. It may be a place where once happiness reigned; now there is nothing but sadness. It may be a place where once there were endearing terms and sweet caresses; now there are hot and bitter words and sharp tongues and broken hearts.

I say, a drunkard's home means something. A drunkard's grave has a definite meaning, too. It will be in the poorer part of the cemetery or it may be in the pauper's ground, the potter's field. But a drunkard's hell has a definite meaning, too. The Bible says that the drunkard shall not inherit the kingdom of God. How many people go to Hell because they drink! I don't mean God can't save a drunkard. The next verses says, "And such were some of you: but ye are washed, but ye are sanctified, but ye are justified." I thank God He saves many a drunkard. I have seen hundreds of them saved.

In Dallas when I was pastor, where we had so many thousands come to Christ, I probably baptized at least one hundred drunkards in our church of seventeen hundred members. Some of the best men in the church were once drunkards. One was Sergeant Simmons of the Dallas police force, but God wonderfully saved him.

Yes, God can save a drunkard. But the trouble is that a man will let this enslave him and turn him away from God, away from the church. Liquor takes him away from the Bible, away from preachers, away from the place of prayer. Liquor takes him away from revival campaigns. If you love it, if the glamour of drink or the slave of drink keeps you away from Jesus Christ, then it will damn your soul.

Oh, repent of your drink, repent of your sins and let Jesus Christ change you! You had better not doubt about this. It is clear, clear that the drunkard shall not inherit the kingdom of God. I don't want you to go to Hell, but my friend, I warn you now, that is where drunkards go.

I was at the University of Chicago doing graduate work. Already I was a college teacher. One night I went down to the Pacific Garden Mission where Mel Trotter, where Billy Sunday, where Harry Monroe, and where many another old drunken bum had been saved—went to do personal work and to sing.

That night when the invitation was given, an old drunk was convicted. He smelled bad, his clothes were filthy, his beard grown, his hair matted, his face dirty—just a drunken bum. But I went and put my arms around him and told him that God loved him. I told him that God would save him if he would trust Jesus Christ. He went with me to kneel down, then he just fell flat on the floor at the front of old P. G. Mission. I never heard a sinner pray as he did. "God, You are my last chance. My wife has left me, I have been kicked out of my job. My children are ashamed of me. They don't want a drunk for a dad. I am going to Hell with nobody to love me, nobody to care, nobody to help me. I am ruined and going to Hell, Jesus, if You don't save me. You are my last chance."

God did save him. He put a song in his heart, sobered him up and made a good, decent man out of him. When I got off my knees from beside that drunken man, now praising God, now praising Him for forgiveness, I never wanted to go back to that college classroom, never wanted to teach any more. I thought: This is the business for me—keeping drunkards out of Hell and putting husbands back in homes and making wives' hearts happy again, giving children back a father, giving industry back good workmen, giving a nation back good citizens, giving God a life out of an old drunken bum. That is better than anything else in the world. I had to preach.

Oh, I have love in my heart for those who have gone into sin. Love causes one to put his arms around a drunkard and talk and pray with him. But if you go on in drink, your heart will become hardened, you will get discouraged, and, worst of all, you will come to the place where you cannot leave it alone. You will be defeated, whipped, enslaved, enamored. You will think it is too late for you; so you will go on in the way of the drunkard. Oh, the slavery of drink that takes a man away from God, away from his wife, away from decency, away from self-control, away from happiness into misery and eternal ruin. You see, drunkard, you will go to Hell if you don't repent. But remember this: Christ has an answer for the drunkard. In Isaiah 1:18 the Scripture says, "Come now, and let us reason together, saith the Lord: though your sins be as scarlet, they shall be as white as snow; though they be red like crimson, they shall be as wool." Bless God for that! Your sins, though they be red as crimson, may be as white as snow.

II. God's Curse on All Who Serve And Promote Drink

Now I come to the second curse —on those who give their neighbor drink. "Woe unto him that giveth his neighbour drink" (Hab. 2:15). Every bartender is under a curse. Every man who owns a saloon, a beer parlor, a winery; every man who has a distillery is under a curse. If you don't believe it, watch the children of the brewers, watch the children of the distillers, watch the children of saloonkeepers and see how they turn out. The Bible says there is a curse on anybody who opens a saloon, on everyone who runs a tavern. There is a curse on everybody who sells it. God says that.

Great revivals such as D. L. Moody had, and Billy Sunday and Charles G. Finney, resulted in the conversion of many saloonkeepers. They are committing a terrible sin and ought to be told about their sin. And we ought to pray that God will convict them. Thank God for all the people who have pled guilty to this crime, who felt the weight of this curse upon them and fled from such a wicked, ungodly business! Everybody who sells liquor—whether it be beer, wine or whisky—is under the curse of making drunkards, paupers and harlots.

The Seller Is Guilty of All the Harm Liquor Does

Then remember again that God here says there is a curse on those who give drink to their neighbor. That means the man who rents the building, too. If you have a building and rent it out and beer is sold there, you are no better than the saloonkeeper. You are a partaker of all the crimes that ever come from booze. If one drinks beer, goes out on the highway and runs his car into a moving train, or runs head-on into a telephone pole, or has a head-on collision, or runs over a pedestrian, you did that—the man who rents out his building for a saloon, a tavern, a honky-tonk, or for a restaurant where beer or wine is sold, or a state liquor store.

The curse, the damnation of God, is on every man who ever sells liquor at all. You may make lots of money now, but it is blood money! Blood money made up of widow's tears, money made up of the bloom of manhood pawned from the cheeks of honest boys who have been led to depravity. It is made up of the purity of girls sold at auction for lewd and lecherous men who like to lead women wrong with liquor. It is blood money, guilt money. The curse of God is on it, and God will bring you to judgment for it, as He will every man who sells liquor, every man who ever makes any profit out of it.

You say, "Brother Rice, it is a legitimate way to make a living." That depends on what you mean. If you think it is legitimate to make drunkards and paupers and harlots. Nobody has to make a living at that price. A man who sells out his country does it for money. The people in the State Department who sold out to Russia, sold our secrets of our defenses to Russia, the atomic bomb secrets, did it for money. And you say you have to have money! I guess you too would betray your country for money. A man who would sell liquor would commit other crimes, because he has no conscience, cares nothing about morality, nor right.

Booze Sellers Are Criminal at Heart

"But it is within the law," you say. It may be within the law of man, but not in the law of God. God Almighty is still going to hold you, the lawbreaker, to account.

"But they are good, self-respecting citizens," you contend. No, they are not, not good citizens, not law-abiding citizens. There never was a state, never was a country where liquor was legalized but what they broke the law. If there was a law about minors, that law was broken if men could do it and get by. If there was a law about the percentage of alcohol, men broke it if they could do it and get by. If there was a law about a certain amount of taxation, they avoided it if they could.

I say, one who doesn't care about breaking a woman's heart, doesn't care whether drink causes somebody to seduce a woman and make a harlot out of a poor innocent girl who drank, wouldn't care about breaking the laws of the land.

I knew a man in Fort Worth, Texas, who was head of the liquor dealer's association of Texas. He told me how, before his conversion, he took a black handbag with $30,000 cash to the Texas State Legislature and how he spent two or three weeks there when a big fight was on to have liquor outlawed in Texas, and how he spent the money to bribe lawmakers, to perjure them, and how he bought their souls and bought their votes the best he could to stop the outlaw of liquor.

I am saying that one who sells liquor is a lawbreaker at heart, a criminal by instinct and by nature. One of my girls could not marry into a family like that. No business partnership is safe with a man like that. I wouldn't trust him in any contract, wouldn't take his word about anything. He is not honest. Anybody who doesn't care about the tears of a broken-hearted woman, nor about little children without clothes in the wintertime; anybody who doesn't care about a man drinking his manhood away until he can't be trusted and loses his job; anybody who doesn't care to bring a home down to poverty, bring a man down to a pauper's grave and a drunkard's Hell—that man is not a good man. The curse of God is on him.

What men will do for drink! The girl who sells her body is a prostitute. She does it for money. But any harlot is as decent as any beer dealer. Any harlot is as good as a man who sells beer in his restaurant. Any harlot is as good as any grocer who sells beer over his counter. A traitor to his country who does it for money has the same kind of motives as you have. You sin to make profit out of the heartbreak and ruin and misery of humankind. God knows you are not fit to live on this earth.

T. DeWitt Talmage well said:

> God knows better than you the number of drinks you have poured out. You keep a list; but a more accurate list has been kept than yours. You may call it Burgundy, Bourbon, Cognac; God calls it strong drink. Whether you sell it in a low oyster cellar or behind the polished counter of first-class hotel, the divine curse is upon you. I tell you plainly that you will meet your customers one day when there will be no counter between you. When your work is done on earth, and you enter the reward of your business, all the souls of the men whom you have destroyed will crowd around you and pour their bitterness into your cup. They will show you their wounds and say, "You made them"; and point to their unquenchable thirst and say, "You kindled it"; and rattle their chain and say, "You forged it." Then their united groans will smite you; and with the hands out of which you once picked the sixpences and shillings they will push you off great precipices while, rolling up from the crags of death, will thunder: "Woe to him that giveth his neighbour drink."

God's Curse on the Hostess Who Serves Alcoholic Drink, Too

Not only is this true about the seller; it is also true about the server.

Perhaps you have cocktails at your house, or beer in the refrigerator, or eggnog at Christmas. Or now and then you have a soothing toddy. Or perhaps it is wine at your formal dinners because you think it is popular, fashionable. Remember, the curse of God is on it. True enough, the red wine is beautiful in the tall stemmed glass; the cut glass looks so beautiful on the white napery, the damask of the table—but remember, God says there is a curse on it. Wait! The wine is the color of blood, and that ought to remind you that its end is death. "Woe unto him that giveth his neighbor drink."

Sometimes it is a casual social glass which makes a drunkard. Sometimes a so-called innocent social glass at a formal dinner, or a glass of beer with "the boys," or an eggnog at Christmas, starts to life a demon that leads later to a man's eternal ruin. Don't do it! There is a curse in that glass. God hates it! Do not serve it in your house. Better to have a rattlesnake or a poisonous adder. These would be labelled "poison." Better have the hooded cobra, or the bushmaster about than wine or liquor. The curse of God is on alcoholic drink and you are guilty of poisoning people when you serve it. You are turning loose the demon in man, turning loose the lust of the carnal nature. You are turning man over to the kind of sin that leads to every other kind of sin. No wonder Shakespeare said:

> What fools men are
> To put this demon in their mouths
> To steal their brains away.

I say right now, a broken home, broken health, a broken heart, a damned soul is what people reap when they sell beer, or serve beer and wine and whisky.

Christians Ought Never Eat Where Beer Is Sold

That isn't all. A lot of you people here don't believe in the liquor business, yet you will eat in a restaurant where it is served, or trade at a store where it is sold. It doesn't bother you you don't drink the beer. So you don't mind making the guy rich who is damning souls. You are glad to put your approval on the dirty bar business. Because you can save two cents on a can of coffee, some of you go down here and trade at a chain store where liquor is sold. It is just as bad as a saloon because it does business under the disguise of respectability.

You say that it is not always convenient to go elsewhere. Not convenient!

I was in Toronto several years ago when the Sword of the Lord put on a great conference on revival and soul winning at Massey Hall. With me were Dr. Bob Jones, Hyman Appelman, Jesse Hendley and other speakers.

One day a good man came and said, "Brother Rice, I want you and Dr. Jones to go with me to dinner."

I thanked him and told him that was kind, but I wanted it understood ahead of time that I never ate where liquor was sold.

"But Brother Rice, in this town you can't get a good meal without going where they sell beer or whisky."

"I didn't say I wanted a good meal. I said I didn't eat where it was sold."

He insisted, "But Brother Rice, it is not convenient. The best places I know of do serve liquor."

"Maybe that is true," I said, "but the best place in town to me is where a decent man can go without compromising his convictions or putting his money and influence back of the liquor business."

After this good brother kept insisting I said firmly, "Will you please drop me off at the Ford Hotel? I would rather eat cheese and crackers in my room than eat in a place where it is sold and sell my soul for somebody's convenience."

"Well, if you insist, I can take you both to the Y. W. C. A. cafeteria. It is not expensive."

We went there and had a meal among some good Christian people. Nobody had the breath of beer around; nobody could ever say that the profit on my dinner encouraged the dirty business of damning souls.

You say, "I go in a drug store where beer is served and get me a malted milk and sandwich, but I do not buy the beer." But your money is backing up everybody who loves the dirty business. Your presence in there says to your children, "It doesn't matter." You are saying, "The saloon or tavern is all right for decent people." But that is a lie. You a lot of you church people are putting your influence back of the people who are breaking down morals, who are turning our girls into harlots, and making our boys into profligates and drunkards. You are putting your money into the kind of thing, and your friendship and your good name behind the kind of thing that has the curse of God upon it. A Christian surely ought to be able to eat somewhere besides in a saloon.

I remind you again that the curse of God is on anybody who gives his neighbor drink, or helps other people give their neighbor drink, or puts his influence behind people who give their neighbor drink.

Voters Who License Beer, Wine and Liquor, Accursed

Not only is the curse of God on the seller and the server, but it is also on the voter. Somebody says, "Well, Brother Rice, I don't think you ought to get into politics." Now don't fret yourself. I probably know better what I ought to do than you.

Somebody else says, "I wouldn't get into politics." But this is still in the Bible. It is still in the Bible that the curse of God is on those who give their neighbor drink. Listen! Anybody who votes in liquor and makes it legal for somebody to advertise it on billboards, advertise it on the radio, advertise it in magazines, advertise it on newspapers, advertise it on street-car cards; anbody who makes it legitimate to put the stink of it under the nostrils of boys and girls as they pass the tavern door, and have it on the menus where decent people go to eat anybody who votes to do that is voting for the Devil, for all the murder, all the adultery, all the crime, all the paupery, all the corruption of government that comes from the dirty booze business! Don't you do it! Don't you ever vote in favor of it.

You say that law won't fix it. Well, law does not fix a lot of things. You have not fixed murder in this country. A lot of people are still being killed in California, and in Illinois, and in New York. But we are not going to repeal the law against murder because somebody now and then commits a murder. You had better bear down and stop it as best you can.

There ought to be a law against selling poison, against inveigling the weak, against overcoming the will of the poor who sometimes do not have the strength they ought to have, and leading people on to be drunkards, paupers, harlots, adulterers, blasphemers and murderers. I say, anybody who does that is guilty before God and is going to pay for it. Do not vote for it!

You thought the New Deal was such a wonderful thing. The Eighteenth Amendment was broken down by a system of propaganda and lie-telling. The United States Government went into the business of making liquor. They went down to the Virgin Islands and spent millions of dollars putting in distilleries.

I passed the window of a liquor store in St. Paul, Minnesota, some years ago. It was piled higher than my head, with layer after layer of bottles of Old Boston Gin. Down in one corner of the labels, in small type, it said, "This gin was made in the Virgin Islands." It was made in distilleries set up by the New Deal Administration, paid for by tax money. The government officially is in the liquor business!

No wonder the curse of God is on Roosevelt's children who cannot live together in peace, with every home of his children broken by divorce. The curse follows them everywhere. I say, there is a curse of God on people who deal in the liquor business. There is a curse of God on the New Deal. No wonder it turned toward socialism, toward communism, toward atheism. When it started out to bring the liquor business back, it was against God and morality. The curse of God is on people who give their neighbor drink.

The curse of God is on the city that takes a rake-off in this ruin of people. The curse of God is on the state that takes a rake-off and makes people pay money to be in the business of making drunkards, paupers and harlots. I say, the curse of Almighty God is on all who have a part in it. You want to remember it.

Christians Could Outlaw Liquor If They Cared

You Baptists and Methodists and Presbyterians and Lutherans, you church members could have run liquor out of this town before now if you had especially cared.

We wonder why we don't have revival. You church people have sold out. You have no convictions, no conscience, no character. No wonder God can't bless you. If you ever stood up for God and right in this matter, then God could hear you when you pray.

It is too bad when it is left to one or two women in the church, a little handful of women in the W. C. T. U. God bless your white ribbon; I have worn a white ribbon. A lot of you others should take a stand along with the little handful of women.

Some preacher may say, "Brother Rice, because you are an evangelist, you can preach that way." Is that so? When I was a pastor I preached this way, too.

When I was pastor of Galilean Baptist Church in Dallas, Texas, I preached on this subject one Sunday night, and I could do it a good deal more pointedly because I could give local references, and don't you doubt but that I did! I called names, and went down the line. I said, "If I ever find anybody in this church who even rents a building where they have a restaurant or where they have a drug store that ever sells a bottle of beer, out you go from this church. We will vote you out first, then you can talk to us about it and repent and try to get back in later." I wouldn't have as a Sunday School teacher nor even one as a member of my church who sold liquor. I said, "Out you go, bag and baggage."

In that tabernacle in Dallas which seated some 1,400, I said, "If anybody doesn't like that, just let me know about it, and I will preach again on it next Sunday night. I will not be the pastor of a church anywhere under Heaven where they take up for the liquor business. Nobody can be a member of my church who makes a business profit out of the damnation of souls in the dirty liquor business." I talked that way when I was pastor.

Some pastor may say, "I might lose my job." Well, you haven't got much of a job, and the church hasn't much of a pastor, if you have no more convictions than that. We need to take sides for Jesus Christ. Christians, particularly preachers, ought to make an issue of morality.

A Personal Experience of the Curse of Drink

"Why is it you are so against liquor?" someone asks. I am against it because it tells me in the Bible to be against it. But it comes closer home than that. I have seen it ruin lots of people. But it comes closer home than that. Let me tell you about it.

Once I was called back to Dundee, the little cowtown in West Texas where I grew up. A young fellow who had three sons and a beautiful wife, a Christian wife (no Christian ought to marry anybody who is not saved, but this woman did) went out on a weekend trip and took with him some bottles of liquor and some home-brew. Yonder on the river bank he and others with him drank and drank. Then he got sick. Liquor often makes people sick. He drank until he was violently sick. The men who were with him brought him back home and called the doctor at Wichita Falls. Intestinal paralysis had been caused by liquor. They rushed him to the hospital for an operation, but he died on the operating table.

I went back there among that family whom I loved. The next afternoon the funeral was held. That young wife nearly died that afternoon. The doctor had to give her a stimulant to keep her heart beating. She was left a widow, with three little fatherless boys to support. All she had was just a little two-room house. With her husband gone, she had no way to make a living. She loved him, but he drank himself to death while he was still young.

That night friends stayed around, so we looked up some bedding for the kinsfolk and others who stayed all night. The young wife said, "There is a mattress out in the garage." It was the same mattress that had been used on this drunken party on the river, when a bunch of men took a big keg of beer, lots of home-brew and whisky, drank, gambled and played poker by the firelight, and when her husband got drunk to his death.

My brother Joe and I unrolled that old mattress. In it was a pint of government liquor and three or four bottles of home-brew. We took them out under the stars on the praries of West Texas and by an old mesquite stump my brother and I stood. Taking one bottle at a time, I held it up before me and God and said, "God, there is a curse on it," then broke the first bottle. I took the second bottle and said, "God helping me, I'll fight it; I'll expose it everywhere I go," then I broke that one. After I had broken them all, we stopped and had prayer, then went back to the house.

That widow was my baby sister!

With a holy hate, I hate the dirty liquor business. I am trying to keep people from the heartbreak of it.

Jesus Is Ready to Forgive and Save You Now

Now listen to me. Drink leads to ruin, to Hell. But, thank God, there is mercy, if you will turn to Jesus Christ. No matter how far you have gone, God loves you still. There is not anywhere God will not follow you. There is not anywhere He cannot help you. There is not anywhere He cannot clean you up. But Jesus will have to do it. Break with the old crowd. Break with the ways of sin. Get out of the hogpen! Prodigal, come on back to the Father's house! God has mercy and forgiveness for you.

I will tell you what all of us need. What you need if you are a drunkard and what you need if you are not a drunkard is Jesus Christ. You need a new heart, need to be born again.

You say, "I will turn over a new leaf." But the new leaf will soon be as dirty as the old leaf. "But," you say, "I'll make up my mind with all my willpower . . . ." Listen, sin takes more than willpower; it takes the grace of God.

You say, "But Brother Rice, I'll change my habits." Even though you may change your habits, you cannot change your heart. Even if you quit your drinking now— if you do, and I hope you will— but if you quit your drinking now, unless you turn to Jesus and repent of your sins and trust Him, you are still a poor, lost soul going to Hell. Don't you see that the only chance for a sinner is to put his trust in Jesus, depend on Him? Tonight let Jesus come into your heart and save your soul.

We have been talking about liquor; now I am turning to a far more important subject than that. What you need is your poor, black heart made white. Some woman is here who never in your life tasted liquor. Somebody is here who is as clean as she can be. But you have a black heart and if you do not get born again, you will go to Hell.

In Romans 3:22, 23 the Scripture says: "For there is no difference: For all have sinned, and come short of the glory of God." There is not any difference, God says. All are sinners alike. The drunkard is a sinner; the man who does not drink is a sinner, too! Harlots are sinners; modest, virtuous women are sinners, too lost sinners, condemned sinners, Hellbound sinners if they are unconverted, if they be not born again, saved by personal trust in Christ.

You can't lick sin without Jesus. You cannot trust your own righteousness. Only the blood of Jesus Christ can save. What you need is a new heart, a new nature. You need to let Jesus come into your heart, forgive your sins, and save your soul today.

And He is ready to do it, too. He said, "God so loved the world, that he gave his only begotten Son, that whosoever believeth in him should not perish, but have everlasting life" (John 3:16). So I beg you to trust Jesus right now to save you. Turn your heart to Him! Repent of your sin. Depend on Him just now to save your soul, by His great mercy! He will do it!

If you are a poor lost sinner, whether a slave to drink or not, will you honestly say yes to God now, definitely deciding now to trust Him as your own Saviour? If so, will you sign the decision form below right now, then copy it in a letter or write me in your own words that you are today taking Christ as your Saviour, depending on Him alone to save you?

Evangelist John R. Rice,
Box 420
Wheaton, Illinois

Dear Brother Rice:

Realizing that I am a poor lost sinner, I today turn from my sin to trust Christ and take Him as my Saviour forever. I have read "The Double Curse of Booze." I believe He is willing to save me, willing to take me, however sinful I have been. I believe He is able to help me do right, able to keep my soul. Here and now I claim Jesus Christ as my Saviour and give Him my heart. I will honestly try to serve Him the rest of my life.

Signed _____

Address _____

_____

Dangerous Triplets

1. Russian Communism
2. New-Deal Socialism
3. Bible-Denying Modernism

How They Are Alike

I am reading tonight from Matthew, chapter 7, beginning with verse 15:

"Beware of false prophets, which come to you in sheep's clothing, but inwardly they are ravening wolves."

You say, "Why all this shouting about modernism?" That is what the Lord said do. He said that false prophets will come who will deceive the people. They will pretend to be sheep, but they are really wolves. So He warned:

"Beware of false prophets, which come to you in sheep's clothing, but inwardly they are ravening wolves. Ye shall know them by their fruits."

One cannot tell a Christian by his fruits because the first fruit, the main fruit of a Christian, is inside, and only God can see the heart. But you can tell a false prophet by his fruit, which is his prophecy—that which he teaches. You can tell a false teacher, and you have a right to judge a false teacher by his fruits, his teaching, the Bible says.

Now begin reading with verse 16:

"Ye shall know them by their fruits. Do men gather grapes of thorns, or figs of thistles?"

There is a book by Nels F. S. Ferre, *Christianity and Society*. Now any intelligent man can read that and judge Ferre by his fruits. He is an infidel. He denies every fundamental of the Christian doctrine. He is a lost sinner. He is of the stripe of Tom Payne, Bob Ingersoll, Voltaire. I can judge him by his fruits. Now I do not know motives and other things of the heart that are not revealed, but when I see a man's fruit, I can judge him if he is a prophet. When he is a prophet, I can judge him by his prophecy, whether he is God's prophet or a false prophet.

"Do men gather grapes of thorns, or figs of thistles? Even so every good tree bringeth forth good fruit: but a corrupt tree bringeth forth evil fruit. A good tree cannot bring forth evil fruit, neither can a corrupt tree bring forth good fruit. Every tree that bringeth not forth good fruit is hewn down, and cast into the fire. Wherefore by their fruits ye shall know them"—Vss. 16-20.

Turn to II Peter, chapter 2, where the same theme is taught:

"But there were false prophets also among the people, even as there shall be false teachers among you, who privily [deceitfully—you will have to watch. They will appear to be sheep, but they are wolves. They will appear to be true preachers, but they are not. They will claim to be angels of light, but they are messengers of darkness.] shall bring in damnable heresies, even denying the Lord that bought them, and bring upon themselves swift destruction."

You ask, "Why do you watch and cry out about modernism?" Because the Lord said we should. He said it would come in, and that we are to watch lest we be deceived about it. Read on:

"And many shall follow their pernicious ways; by reason of whom the way of truth shall be evil spoken of."

What is the motive of the communists, the modernists, the socialists, false prophets and cults?

"And through covetousness shall they with feigned words [deceitful words, lying words] make merchandise of you: whose judgment now of a long time lingereth not, and their damnation slumbereth not."

Damnable heresies. The passage I read said that every tree that doesn't bring forth good fruit, judged by doctrine—that tree shall be cut down and cast in the fire. Here He said of false prophets that "their judgment now of a long time lingereth not, and their damnation slumbereth not." The people God is talking about here are going to Hell. They pretend to be Christians, pretend to be for God, pretend to be ministers, but they are poor lost sinners and their damnation slumbereth not. They are going quickly to Hell.

Someone says, "I don't like your calling these men names and saying things about them." The Bible said things about them, and I won't say anything about anybody unless I can prove that by his fruits he is a denier of Christ and that these words in the Scriptures were about him.

First of all, I will define communism, then define socialism, showing how the Bible opposes Communism, and how socialism and communism are really the same essentially in foundation and doctrine. Then I will show how modernism is like them both.

WHAT COMMUNISM ACTUALLY TEACHES

First, I will set out to define communism.

I have here in my hand a sermon by Dr. V. Raymond Edman, President of Wheaton College. This sermon was used in THE SWORD OF THE LORD in 1954. It is titled, "The Big Lie," and it is a sermon on communism. He gives the Scripture about strong delusions, that they should believe a lie, and he says communism is "The Big Lie."

Now about Karl Marx, the founder of the doctrine of communism, Dr. Edman says:

"It must be remembered that Karl Marx was a theorist, a doctrinaire economist, with no practical experience in the ideas which he propagated. He never earned a day's wages in his life. Once he applied for employment in an office, but his handwriting was so wretched that he was immediately discharged. He lived by the largesse of others. He lived aloof, isolated, even from them who supported him out of their poverty. He was insensitive to the interests of others, irritable in the extreme, inconsiderate of everyone. Even his admiring biographers had to admit that he was 'morbidly thin-skinned and jealously suspicious of the least sign of antagonism to his person or his doctrine.'"

1. Communism Is Against Private Ownership of Property

Karl Marx was no friend of the working man, though he claimed to be. Dr. Edman says further:

"What are the basic communist economic principles? Karl Marx states them very graphically, with frankness that is brutal, in his *Communist Manifesto*, in which he says:

"*'The theory of the communists may be summed up in the single sentence: Abolition of private property.'*"

That quotation is from Karl Marx in *Communist Manifesto*. Marx goes on to say:

"You are horrified at our intending to do away with private property . . . in one word, you reproach us with intending to do away with your property. Precisely so; that is just what we intend."

Communism sets out to do away with private property, to seize people's property, and whether they do it by law or whether they do it without law, literally to rob people of their property, to abolish private property.

I quote from Dr. Edman's sermon:

"To achieve this abolition of private property so that everything is owned corporately by the State, a communist program was proposed by Marx. He declared that 'The proletariat will use its political supremacy to wrest, by degrees, all capital from the bourgeoisie, to centralize all instruments of production in the hands of the State;' and to that end the communists plan:

"*1. 'Abolition of property in*

land and application of all rents of land to public purposes.'"

Notice, all property in land is to be turned over to the State, little by little, to be wrested, twisted, stolen, robbed, confiscated from people and taken by the State.

"2. 'A heavy progressive or graduated income tax.'"

Now note carefully. I'll refer to that again. This is a communist proposal. What is the purpose? To steal the property of people and put it into the hands of the State. And one method? "A heavy progressive or graduated income tax."

"3. 'The abolition of all right of inheritance.'"

You may begin to see some likeness to the New Deal program. "Abolition of all right of inheritance." If the lands cannot go to sons, if the property cannot go to daughters, it can be confiscated in inheritance taxes by the State. "The abolition of private property." This is the communist method of doing it. Again,

"4. 'Confiscation of the property of all emigrants and rebels [by "emigrants and rebels" was meant citizens who would flee from a communist State].'"

All the people who couldn't stand that, their lives in danger, would flee and the government would take their property. Quoting again,

"5. 'Centralization of credit in the hands of the State, by means of a national branch with State capital and an exclusive monopoly; and furthermore the socialization of transportation.'"

That is, taking over the railroads, the bus lines, air lines. Factory production—seizing all the factories, all the mills. Agriculture—seizing all the farms, all the ranches, all the gardens.

Dr. Edman continues his quote from Marx:

"'. . . and concluding with what already has long since been available, "Free education for all children in public schools."'"

That part we have had from many, many years back in America.

Now, do you know what the program of communism is? The abolition of private property, getting a dictatorship of some working people over the people who have owned property and have been bosses and have been owners and have been managers and foremen, then little by little steal or "wrest"—the word Marx uses—or rob from people all private property—all their lands, all their mills, all their garages, all their stores, all the means of production, all the railroads, all the mines.

2. Communism Would Destroy Freedom of the Individual

I'll go a little further now. As well as the abolition of private property, it plans the destruction of individual freedom.

Karl Marx again speaks:

"The abolition of this state of things is called by the bourgeoisie, abolition of individuality and freedom! And rightly so."

Quoting Karl Marx:
"The abolition of bourgeois in-

dividually, bourgeois independence, and bourgeois freedom, is undoubtedly aimed at."

That is this: Let us get a few working people and put them in charge, make them dictators, and we intend, he says, to take the freedom away from everybody who owns any property, as well as their profits. I'll not go further into it, though there is much more. But the plan is to put them in the greatest bondage possible.

Here is another word. Another quotation. Dr. Edman says:

"To that end the bases of society must be destroyed. First, the 'individual . . . the middle-class owner of property . . . must, indeed, be swept out of the way.' "

3. Communism Would Abolish the Family As We Know It

Next comes the family. The *Communist Manifesto* becomes savage in what it says about the family. Karl Marx, the founder of communism, the founder of socialism, says again,

"Abolition of the family! . . . The bourgeois family will vanish as a matter of course when its complement vanishes, and both will vanish with the banishing of capital . . . . The bourgeois claptrap about the family and education, about the hallowed co-relation of parent and child, becomes all the more disgusting . . . by the action of Modern Industry."

Then Marx goes on to say,

"The community of women, [that is, making women the property of everybody and passing the women around]; it has existed almost from time immemorial."

That is already being done, he says, but we will legalize it. Now that is communism according to the author himself, Karl Marx, as quoted from the *Communist Manifesto*.

HOW BIBLE OPPOSES COMMUNISM IN PRINCIPLES

Now let us take the Bible and show some things wrong with communism. Without trying to touch on all, here are a few. The Bible is out-and-out against communism, and in a bit you will see why communism is atheistic, why communism cannot be Christian.

1. The Bible Teaches Private Ownership of Property

First, the ownership of property, private property, is taught in the Bible. It is not only a right of people but it is a spiritual plan of God. Someone says, "The churches, the modernists say—Bishop Oxnam says, Nels F. S. Ferre says, and other men say—that Christianity must not be tied up with any system of economics." But the Bible has a system of economics. Turn to Exodus, chapter 20, to find God's plan about ownership of property. He said in verse 15, "Thou shalt not steal." Now, there are some things that are inviolate if one follows the Bible. The private ownership of property—"Thou shalt not steal."

Not only "Thou shalt not steal," but property ownership is the only matter in the Ten Commandments, as far as I know, that is mentioned twice. He says, "Thou shalt not covet thy neighbour's house, thou shalt not covet thy neighbour's wife, nor his manservant, nor his maidservant, nor his ox, nor his ass, nor any thing that is thy neighbour's." Nothing could be clearer than that God intended people to own property, to own land, to own oxen, to own asses, and it should be undisturbed, that it would be a sin even for people to covet what belongs to somebody else. So every communist is a thief because he wants what does not belong to him, what he did not earn.

I'll go further: Every socialist and New Dealer is crooked because he violates this plain command of God to covet for himself money that somebody else earned, but he wants it and he promises to vote a New Deal ticket if he gets it. Yes, socialism and communism are against the plain Bible teaching that it is wrong to take what belongs to somebody else, it is wrong to covet what belongs to somebody else.

Again in Exodus 22, the Scripture says, "If a man shall steal an ox, or a sheep, and kill it, or sell it; he shall restore five oxen for an ox, and four sheep for a sheep." That's pretty drastic, isn't it? Yes, but God is saying, 'I want you to see that there is something that is inviolate.' You cannot disturb the Bible law of private ownership without sinning against God. If it is an ox, you restore five times; if it is a sheep, you restore four times. Then God goes on to say that if a thief be found breaking in at night and you knock him in the head and kill him, you will be blameless.

You say, "I don't think so much of property rights as I do of human rights." But property ownership is a human right. And God requires it. Any philosophy of government that violates this plain order of God—that people may earn or buy property and own it; people may buy it and keep it and use it, and may reap from it, and may invest in it, and earn from the investment—any philosophy that is against that, is against the Bible plan.

Why do Americans prosper? Because the American Constitution is primarily based upon such certain fundamental laws that are God's laws. It was no accident that the founders of our country put on the dollar, "In God We Trust." It is no accident that we inaugurate a man as President by having him kiss the Bible. It is no accident that we have a chaplain pray every time Congress opens, every time the Senate opens. It is no accident that we have set out to have a chaplain for every group of soldiers and on every major battleship, to pray and preach the Gospel and stand for God. Yes, our forefathers wanted a country based on God's law.

That is the reason Americans are the best paid, have more to eat, enjoy more conveniences, are more advanced, have more leisure, —more of everything. We have a country that started out on God's plan, and God blessed it. Now some nuts would like to throw it away.

2. Nothing Like Marxist Communism in Jerusalem Church

Now about this matter of communism. "Brother Rice, didn't they have communism in Jerusalem?" "Don't you think they had communism in Acts, chapter 4 and 5?" someone may ask. Well, let me read it—Acts, chapter 4, beginning with verse 34:

"Neither was there any among them that lacked: for as many as were possessors of lands or houses sold them, and brought the prices of the things that were sold, And laid them down at the apostles' feet: and distribution was made unto every man according as he had need. And Joses, who by the apostles was surnamed Barnabas, (which is, being interpreted, The son of consolation,) a Levite, and of the country of Cyprus, Having land, sold it, and brought the money, and laid it at the apostles' feet."

Now as many as had land, the multitude of them that believed, were of one heart, and one soul. Verse 32, "Neither said any of them that ought of the things which he possessed were his own; but they had all things common."

"Wasn't that communism?" you ask. Three or four things are to be said. First, this was a voluntary arrangement of a group of Christians. It didn't include anybody else—only some Christians who wanted to do it, like a group of Christians who get together at a country church and have dinner on the ground. Isn't that all right? It was voluntary.

Notice this other thing: It was an emergency measure never intended for wider use. It is never commanded in the Bible anywhere, and this is the only community in the New Testament where it ever happened, as far as we know. And in this case, it brought disaster, and it wasn't long until Paul had to go up and down the Roman Empire and raise money, for they all went busted and everybody had to be fed on public charity. Isn't that right? This is no example, then, of communism.

Notice these are all Christians. What they did, they did voluntarily, and even so, it didn't work. It was not commanded. They meant well; maybe it was an emergency. Since there were so many new converts, so many people being arrested, so many people getting in jail, perhaps it was all right to sell all the land and feed everybody. But then somebody is going to have to take up a collection from people still working and making a living and owning the property, to take care of it. And that's what they did. No communism there.

Go a little further. Here in the next chapter are Ananias and Sapphira:

"But a certain man named Ananias, with Sapphira his wife, sold a possession, and kept back part of the price, his wife also being privy to it, and brought a certain part, and laid it at the apostles' feet. But Peter said, Ananias, why hath Satan filled thine heart to lie to the Holy Ghost?"

What was his sin? Not the sin of holding back the money, but a sin of lying and pretending to be giving everything, like Barnabas did in the Scripture just above it. Peter said, "Why hath Satan filled thine heart to lie to the Holy Ghost, and to keep back part of the price of the land? Whiles it remained, was it not thine own?" In other words, "It was yours. You didn't have to sell it. Nobody told you to. God didn't require you to give it. It was your own. After it was sold, was it not in thine own power? After you sold the land and had the money, you didn't have to bring it. But you did wrong to lie to God about it and lie to the people about it; so God is going to teach you a lesson." So God knocked him over dead and the young men carried him out.

Do you see what I'm talking about? The Bible all the way through is for private ownership of property. That is a clear Bible principle. Private ownership of property.

3. Investment and Interest on Invested Capital Approved by Jesus

Let's go a little further. The proposition, clear in the Bible also, which is denied by modernists, it's a part of the free enterprise system, is the right to have money, and to save money, and get interest on your money, the right to invest in a business, or in a factory, or in notes, or in stocks or bonds, to invest and to get interest on the money. In Matthew, chapter 25, Jesus gives this story of the talents, verse 24:

"Then he which had received the one talent came and said, Lord, I knew thee that thou art an hard man, reaping where thou hast not sown, and gathering where thou hast not strawed: And I was afraid, and went and hid thy talent in the earth: lo, there thou hast that is thine."

A talent—how much was it? In silver, close to $2,000. In gold, close to $32,000. A talent is a certain measurement of money. "Now, I left you a talent; why didn't you use it?" He said: "His Lord answered and said unto him, Thou wicked and slothful servant, thou knewest that I reap where I sowed not, and gather where I have not strawed: Thou oughtest therefore to have put my money to the exchangers [invested in a bank, or invested in a loan trust] and then at my coming I should have received mine own with usury."

Now Jesus Christ Himself was talking, and He said that it is proper and right to invest your money and get interest on your money. Communism, then, is against the Bible. Anybody is against the Bible who tries to shut off investing because a man has money. He saved it, he worked for it, he put it by, he was thrifty, while a lot of you other people would go on relief, while you went out to the night spots and spent it in luxury and riotous living.

I'm having to pay taxes to keep some of you deadbeats up down here in Tennessee because you want to use electricity that the rest of us pay for. I helped to pay a billion and a half dollars on the TVA proposition, to put it in. So it doesn't have to pay taxes and so you people down here in the Tennessee area get electricity which you do not pay for, but ride the rest of the United States because you pay less than it cost. Aren't you proud of that, you people on relief?

4. God's Plan for Inheritance of Wealth and Property

Now, again, the Bible has a clear word about inheritance. Listen, the Scripture tells us that Abraham had flocks and herds and much riches and he left it all to Isaac. He gave a settlement to Ishmael and sent him away. He gave a settlement to other sons after he married Keturah, and sent them away. Then the great bulk of his estate, the Scripture says, he gave to Isaac. That is an inheritance in a Bible pattern. The Bible tells us how David had accumulated great wealth and left it in the hands of King Solomon so that Solomon was one of the richest men who ever lived. Inheritance.

That isn't all. The land of Palestine was cut up according to families and it was the law and the rule that the land, the farms, the estates should be handed down father to son, to grandson, to great grandson, year after year. And Leviticus, chapter 25, goes into a great deal of detail to show us how that if a man fall on hard days and has to sell his inheritance, within a year's time he can go and redeem it back, because God is saying it is proper and right and it is good for society that the inheritance should pass from father to son.

Now Karl Marx's idea, and the New Deal idea in America—that gifts and taxes and inheritance taxes should take all that a man has earned away from him and his heirs to buy votes with from the common people who want a free ride, and will be glad to vote for a man that will give them more—is wrong. I say, that idea is not of God. It was Karl Marx's idea, which he got from the Devil. The Bible is for inheritance and passing on of property to sons.

5. The Bible Teaches the Great Principle of Sowing and Reaping, Earning and Getting

Here is another matter. How does the Bible differ from communism? There is a divine law of sowing and reaping which communism and socialism ignore. What is this law in the Bible? "Whatsoever a man soweth, that shall he also reap." The divine law is, "They that sow in tears shall reap in joy. He that goeth forth and weepeth bearing precious seed, shall doubtless come again with rejoicing, bringing his sheaves with him." What you sow you have a right to reap. If you sow sin, you are going to reap trouble.

What is the communist's plan? "From each according to his ability, and to each according to his need." Not to each according as he has earned, but to each according to his need. You see, communism changes God's divine law. Divine law is sow and reap. If one earns more money, he ought to get more money. If one works harder, he ought to get a raise. The fellow who does not work as much ought to be fired. That is divine law.

Paul said in II Thessalonians 3, 'I've written to you that there are some who are busybodies, working not at all and causing trouble. All right, let such eat his own bread. When I was there before, I told you that if any would not work, neither should he eat.' Hard boiled? No, that's just a matter of right and wrong. That is just sowing and reaping. That is the divine law. That is why there is a Hell for Christ-rejecting sinners. That is why there is a reward for soul winning. That is why, when a man works hard, he can make a better crop. That is why the man who works harder and studies more, advances and gets to own the business. That is God's law, not man's. What you call capitalism is another way of saying that what you sow, you reap; another way of saying God blesses hard work, and faith, and enterprise, and intelligence, and self-sacrifice. But divine law? Communism is against it, socialism is against it.

6. It Is Not Wrong to Save, to Invest, to Get Wealth

Let us see another thing here, another way. The Bible says riches and honor properly come to people who serve God. Proverbs, chapter 3 verses 9 and 10:

"Honour the Lord with thy substance, and with the firstfruits of all thine increase: So shall thy barns be filled with plenty, and thy presses shall burst out with new wine."

I'll show you that socialism and communism have the same root, have the same creed. I'll show you in a moment, but right now I want you to see that socialism and communism say that for a man to earn more money is wrong, that the fellow with the muscles and the fellow who wants only a 30-hour week ought to have just as much as the fellow who schemes and plans and stays awake at night and works 16 hours a day, and so on. He says that the one ought to have as much as the other. The Bible doesn't say that. The communist says that there is no difference, and that since there is no God any how, it is to everybody according to his needs. But the Bible says, "Honour the Lord with thy substance, and with the firstfruits of all thine increase: So shall thy barns be filled with plenty, and thy presses shall burst out with new wine." A divine law of sowing and reaping. A divine law of wealth. A divine law, that it is an honor to earn more money, to make good in this world, to save money, and take care of your family.

The communistic and socialistic plan is that everybody more or less is on relief. A paternal state, a welfare state, with some laboring people in charge of it, everybody dipping into the fund so you can keep them in line, so you can buy their votes, and tell them what to do, etc.

What is the Bible plan? Take care of your own people. Paul said to Timothy, 'If anyone has a mother, or an aunt, or a widow to take care of, don't bring her to the church. You requite your own parents.' Then comes that famous Scripture which is nearly always quoted out of context, "If any provide not for his own, and specially for those of his own house [the widows of his own household, his own widowed mother or aunt, or old-maid sister, or somebody else who needs support of his own family], he hath denied the faith, and is worse than an infidel."

This socialistic idea that the government has to take care of all the old people, has to take care of everybody when the work runs out, and so on, is against the Bible plan. The Bible plan is, "Honour thy father and thy mother." Don't you think there are some people who need to be taken care of? Yes, and Paul goes on to say in I Timothy, "Let not a widow be taken into the number if she is less than sixty years old." Any woman under sixty will try to marry again anyhow, if she gets a chance! And a woman past sixty could be persuaded! But let a widow not be taken unless she has been married only to one husband, and if she have washed the saints' feet, if she has been good in taking in strangers, has been charitable, and so on. It is all right for society to support that kind of a woman, if she is past sixty and has been married only once, and lived for God, a faithful Christian woman, and if she has no child to support her. That is the ordinary way, the American way, what we call capitalism, the free enterprise way. Do you see the difference from that and socialism, and communism?

SOCIALISM AND COMMUNISM ALIKE

Now what do we mean by socialism? Let me define socialism. I have here a book, *Labor and Tomorrow's World*, by Bishop G. Bromley Oxnam, Methodist bishop in Washington, D. C., the most important diocese of all of Methodism.

Socialism, Just Like Communism, Says Do Away With Private Ownership of Property and Business

On page 90 Dr. Oxnam tells us what socialism is. This is an authoritative statement. He is a socialist, and favors it, and knows what it is.

"In a little volume now more than thirty years old entitled *Socialism Summed Up*, Morris Hillquit set forth the essential position of the socialist with exceptional lucidity. He says: 'The Socialists demand that the principal industries of the nation, the business of providing the necessaries of life, be conducted by the community for the benefit of its members.'"

And then he says:

"Stated in more concrete terms, the Socialist program requires the public or collective ownership and operation of the principal instruments and agencies for the production and distribution of wealth the land, mines, railroads, steamboats, telegraph and telephone lines, mills, factories and modern machinery. [That takes in most of it, doesn't it? What about that, that they are not to be privately owned but to be owned by the government? That is socialism.—Ed.]

"This is the main program and the ultimate aim of the whole Socialist movement, and the political creed of all Socialists. It is the unfailing test of Socialist adherence, and admits of no limitation, extension or variation. Whoever accepts this program is a Socialist; whoever does not, is not."

What is the program? Public ownership of all the principal instruments and agencies, production, distribution of wealth, the land, the mines, railroads, all the farms, all the factories, all the shops, steamboat, telegraph, telephone lines, mills, factories, and modern machinery. No private ownership. That is socialism. You ask the difference between that and communism. No difference in the creed. The only difference is that communism, as it is in Russia, insists on the right to do it with a violent overthrow, bloodshed, and murder, while the socialists say, "No, let us get in and do it in America. We can get Huey Long, or Roosevelt, and little by little fool the people to keep giving more of other people's money so we can get enough votes and we take things away and change the income tax, and change inheritance tax, and put on confiscatory income taxes on the higher bracket, then it won't be long until we have all the rich people poor, and the poor people will be in charge, the ones who didn't earn it." You see, there is no difference in the creed. The only difference is whether you kill somebody to do it, or whether you do it without killing.

Who is the father of communism? Karl Marx. Who is the father of socialism? Karl Marx. You know what the name of Russia is? Russia is the *Soviet Union of Socialist Republics*. What is Russia? A socialist state. No difference in socialism and communism.

Why Communists and Socialists Turn Up Together: They Agree

How many have ever read the book, *The Witness*? Whittaker Chambers in that book tells how strange it is that New Dealers in some naive way can't recognize the communists. President Roosevelt just could not believe that Alger Hiss was a communist and betraying his country. He just could not believe that Dexter White was a communist and betraying his country. He kept promoting him and kept whacking everybody who raised his head to defend America from communism.

Now why? Because fundamentally the real reason is that there was kinship of spirit, and so they believed alike—the one a communist and the other a socialist. They say, "Take the money away from the man who earns it and give it to the fellow who does not earn it. Take over things by the government; let the government run everything; don't let anybody make very much money. And be sure to keep enough at hand to pass out to buy votes with, buy the farmers by giving them money to plow up what they planted, or pay them more than they could get on the law of supply and demand on the natural markets," etc. But always the same principle—take it over, own it by the state, use it for political purposes, buy the votes, buy the people, put over a program with it, and finally end up in a dictatorship.

Now there is no difference in the eventual end of the socialists and the communists. The communists say, "Let us kill people and get them out of the way and do it now." The socialists say, "No, let us do it a little slower and easier. Don't kill them if we can help it." I'm not lying, nor joking, nor twisting, but giving you the facts about it.

Why is there a kinship? Why is it? Here a man says, "I'm against communism." But what he means is, "I'm against Russia." But, he says, "I'd like to make America like Russia." E. Stanley Jones would say, "Oh, I'm against communism." But he would say, "I mean, of course, Russian communism. But I'd like to help get America to be a collective state like Russia." Do you see?

HOW MODERNISM FITS THE SOCIALIST-COMMUNIST PROGRAM

Here is a book, *Labor in Tomorrow's World,* by G. Bromley Oxnam—"A distinguished interpretation of the labor movement in relation to the world-wide mission of the Christian church." You will be interested to know that this book is dedicated to Francis John McConnell, the most radical modernist of the Methodist church, now retired, and who, I believe, recently died.

Here is another book, *Preaching and the Social Crisis,* edited by G. Bromley Oxnam, and this has a great many series of lectures delivered for the Boston University School of Theology. Contents:

"Preaching and Socialism," by Kirby Page;

"Communism's Challenge to Christianity," by Jerome Davis;

"Preaching and the Industrial Order," by Harry Frederick Ward, the man who started the Methodist Social Action Committee and sworn before Congress to be a communist, a professor in Union Theological Seminary and the teacher and mentor of Bishop Oxnam himself. Dr. Oxnam used to be his secretary;

"Preaching and the Race Problem," by William Nelson DeBerry;

"The Preacher and Revolution," by G. Bromley Oxnam; and other chapters by Francis McConnell, Burris Atkins Jenkins, etc., more of the same kind.

Do you remember the method that Karl Marx said that communism should use to take property away from the people and to get it in the hands of a dictatorship? Listen and I'll read you his statements. Here they are:

"1. Abolition of private property in land and application of all rents of lands to public purposes:

2. A heavy progressive or graduated income tax."

Now, why, if one man, beyond a certain low limit, so a man will have a chance, beyond that, why not everybody 10% or everybody 20%? No, because the man who made more money may want to take it away from you, Marx says, so let us get 90% of his while we get 20% of somebody else. So says Marx and some other people you've heard about. All right, listen now.

"3. The abolition of all right of inheritance."

Let's take it away in taxes instead of letting a man give it to his children.

"4. The confiscation of the property of all emigrants and rebels," those who may have left the State. "5. Centralization of credit in the hands of the State, . . . furthermore, the socialization of transportation, factory production, agriculture."

We're pretty far gone toward that in agriculture now. I'm just reminding you of how closely alike are communism and socialism. Those are two of the triplets that are fairly to be called members of the same party!

Modernists Openly Avow Socialism

We go a little further. How are modernism, communism, and socialism alike? Now, I think I have showed you there would be no doubt that communism and socialism are alike. But now how is modernism like socialism and communism? Here are the facts. For example, this book by G. Bromley Oxnam on *Preaching and the Social Crisis* is not about the Gospel, is not the plan of salvation, is not what the Bible teaches us, but is about preaching and the social crisis of turning everything that we can into socialism in this country. Now, why would that have to be by a Methodist preacher and why would three of the sermons in here be by Methodist bishops? On page 19 I read in this book by a modernist preacher. See if you think this is socialism or not. This sermon is by Kirby Page, edited by Bishop Oxnam:

"It is supremely tragic that at this late day evidence must still be produced that Socialism is much closer akin to Christian gospel than capitalism."

That isn't so, but that's what he says. So he's a socialist, isn't he? All right, quoting again from page 19:

"For the Christian Church to disentangle itself from the meshes of capitalism [the American free enterprise system, private ownership of property] is as crucial and urgent in our time as it was for the church of our fore fathers' day to break with slavery."

Another quotation, page 32. Are modernist preachers socialist and communist? Listen carefully now:

"Surely, it is obvious that the co-operative method of Socialism is much closer akin to Jesus' way of life than is the competitive combat of capitalism."

So Kirby Page said, with Bishop Oxnam's approval.

Here is another one. On page 38, Jerome Davis, a famous modernist and socialist, says in this book, edited by Bishop Oxnam:

"They demand a dictatorship of producers. They [the communist leaders] believe it is possible to own, control and use all property for the benefit of the workers through a system of state Socialism."

You see, they know socialism and communism are the same.

"Nothing must be run for the profit of the individual; everything must be run in the interests of the masses—the real producers. Production must be for use and not for profit. Furthermore, they demand that all property relations be humanized; that we must revolutionize factory conditions in the interests of the workers. All income must be socialized. [Nobody's income according to his work, but according to what the State decrees, you see?] The effort of everyone in society shall be planned and directed for the common good."

No one will work where he wants to; he works where he is told. Nobody to get what he agrees and bargains to work for; he will get what the State, run by dictators, tells him he can get. Now, that statement is by Jerome Davis, modernist preacher, and edited by Bishop G. Bromley Oxnam of Washington, D. C., the most prominent bishop of the Methodist Church and one of the presidents of the World Council of Churches.

Modernist Leaders Say They Are Leaders in Socialist-Modernist Revolution

Here is another one, another quotation by Jerome Davis on page 55:

"As ministers of Jesus Christ, we must recognize again that we are leaders in a revolutionary movement . . . ."

Well, then, what is the Methodist Church training preachers for? To be leaders in a revolutionary movement. What is the National Council of Churches insisting that preachers do? To be leaders in a revolutionary movement. Listen now. ". . . which is seeking nothing short of the complete overthrow of special privilege [that is, a man keeping what he earns], economic selfishness [I'll earn it and I'll get paid for it], and racial discrimination." This involves not only a revolution of the human heart but a revolution of the social order.

Change the American way of life to the Russian way of life. Socialism. Communism.

How Modernists and Communists Are Alike in Being Against the Bible

Now, why is it that G. Bromley Oxnam, for example, admitted before the Investigating Committee of Congress, that he had joined nine different communist-front organizations? Note, he did not say he was a communist, and nobody accused him of being a communist, but if he were a communist, he wouldn't tell it. I don't know; I don't say that. But he admitted that he had joined nine different organizations which, it turned out, had been organized by communists and for communist aims in America. Now, why is it that modernists run with that crowd? And those that are not red are pink. I want to show you why they are alike.

Listen carefully. First of all, they start alike against the Bible. The communists hate the Bible. The communists say that all religion is the opiate of the people. They start alike in that they do not believe the Bible. The modernist doesn't believe the Bible. They say, "We will not have that authority." The communist says, "We will not have the Bible as authority." The socialist says, "We will not have that Bible as authority." Does anybody know why as soon as we got a pro-socialist New-Deal government in this country, we repealed the Eighteenth Amendment? The Bible standards do not fit with socialism and communism.

They are alike in that they all reject the Bible. Listen to me! Don't put a modernist in with Christians. Put him with infidels The man who does not believe that the Bible is true, does not believe that Jesus was born of a virgin, who believes that the Bible is a book of myths and legends as well as some good things, and who does not believe in the atoning blood, that man is not a Christian, but is an infidel! He is an unbeliever! You rate a modernist not with Christians but with communists and with infidels, with Tom Payne, with Bob Ingersol, with Voltaire. On all the principal essentials they agree exactly. Yes. Now do you see why they are alike?

Modernists, Like Communism, Have a Philosophy Based on Evolution, Not Supernatural Creation

Second, they are alike on evolution. Modernists believe that the world came not by direct creation of God, but by evolution; that man came by slowly evolving from lower forms of life. They trace man from apes on back to one-celled animals, etc. They believe that man came by evolution. But that is a part of the particular doctrine of Karl Marx. And to whom did Karl Marx dedicate his book, *Communist Manifesto?* To Charles Darwin! Yes. He says that the human race is evolving upward and that therefore, little by little, society is growing into a better state and eventually we will not have any private property, and everybody will own everything together. And he says that evolution is absolutely certain to bring communism over the whole world. So Stalin taught, so all communists believe. So you believe when you believe in evolution instead of direct creation by God, when you believe not that God's Bible is authoritative, but that just whatever will work out to fit your scheme is all right.

Modernists, Like Communists and Socialists, Exalt Man As Good

Do you see the difference? Now third, modernists, evolutionists, socialists, all believe alike on the creation of man. The Bible says that man was created in God's image but fell, that man is a fallen creature, that the heart is desperately wicked, that a man must be born again or go to Hell, that man is an enemy of God, estranged from God from the womb. But modernism says, "No." They said, "Man [Christian Science puts it this way too] is the unfallen son of God." The modernist declares that there is good in every man. He says God is the father of all and that all are brothers. He says men do not need to be born again—he is already born of God. I have a book by Harry Emerson Fosdick, *The Hope of the World,* in which he says in a sermon on "The Peril of Worshipping Jesus," "Do you believe that Jesus is divine? Yes," he said, "I do, like my mother was divine." Is he blaspheming?

Now, communist, socialist, modernist, *all* agree that man is essentially good, and it is just the system that is wrong. If man had a chance he would come out all right. Do you see why modernists turn naturally to socialism? Do you know why the modernist or liberal will be working for a collective state and for uniting all the churches, and uniting world government, and everybody getting together to own the property collectively instead of private enterprise? Because he does not believe what the Bible says about man, but he believes man is essentially good, like the socialists and the communists believe! The modernists and the socialists and communists all come out alike on that matter. Do you see why they run together? They do not always know why, but it turns out that way because they are alike. They have the same doctrinal background.

The Deceitful Morality of Communism and Modernism Alike

Fourth, the modernists and the communists are alike in a certain wicked immorality. The Bible declares that with feigned words these modernists will make merchandise of you. ". . . with deceitful words," the Scripture says. They are false prophets come to you in sheep's clothing. They are wolves in sheep's clothing. What do you mean? They are pretending to be sheep, but they are wolves. They are pretending to be preachers of the Gospel, but they are infidels. They will come as angels of light, Paul said, but they are enemies of your souls, and they are wicked spirits. Do you see what the Bible teaches?

A communist says, "I don't agree with the Bible, so I am not bound by the Ten Commandments." He says, "There is no God, so there is no morality, and there's nobody holding me to account. If I can get by with it, I'll get by with it." There is no right and wrong to a communist except, "What will advance communism and what will not?" If lying will win, if murder will win, if stealing will win, if rape will win, that is all right. The communists have no morality. A man is a fool to trust Russia because Russian leaders are all communists, which means they will tell as big a lie as they want to. They've no conscience on it. They say if it prospers Russia, and if it prospers communism, then it is right to lie.

What about a modernist? What do you think about a modernist who comes in and is ordained as a Baptist preacher and says that he agrees with the New Hampshire Confession of Faith. "What do you believe? Were you converted? What do you believe about the inspiration of the Bible? What do you believe about Hell? What do you believe about the blood atonement? How do you believe people are saved?" Are preachers asked those questions still? Now what about a Baptist preacher who says he believes the Bible, says he believes the virgin birth, believes Jesus rose from the dead, says he believes man is a sinner and must be born again, but takes those vows tongue in cheek, then little by little sets out to break down faith and to deny the Bible that he promised God and men he would support?

A Methodist preacher wrote me, and I answered his letter just today, "I wish you would have that SWORD OF THE LORD stopped. I don't want it coming to my place." And he said some mean things. I wrote him that I would stop the paper whom someone sent him because they loved him. But I asked him, "Why don't you be honest about it and say, 'The truth is, I am against the historic Christian position; I do not believe the Bible; I despise the Christ presented in THE SWORD OF THE LORD'? Why don't you say that instead of running me down and accusing me of being a trouble-maker?" I went on to say, "You were ordained, and every Methodist preacher who is ordained once took solemn vows that he believes the Articles of Religion of the Methodist Church which are unchanged down through the years. And you vowed publicly to teach them and defend them. Now, then, suppose you took them tongue in cheek. Never mind; you will meet God and give an account. Yes, we will stop THE SWORD OF THE LORD but what can an honest man do when he finds he is not a Christian and is against historic Christianity and against the Christ of the Bible and he is pretending to be a Gospel minister?"

I am saying there is a fundamental kinship of immorality and deceit and wickedness with a man who is a modernist, just like the man who is a communist. Isn't it terrible that men should creep in and try to steal secrets and betray the United States Government? Yes. Well, what is the difference for a man to teach in Louisville Seminary, supported by honest Baptist money, and there break down faith of young men in the inspiration of the Bible, knowing he is paid by the sacrificial gifts of common Baptists who believe it all? That is as fundamentally wicked as murder. Yes sir!

Do you see that communists and modernists are of the same stripe? They are wicked, rebellious sinners, against God and against Christ, against the Bible and against Bible morality and Bible doctrine and Bible truth. They are triplets—communism, socialism, modernism.

FOR THE CHRISTIAN IT MUST BE CHRIST AND THE WHOLE BIBLE OR NOTHING

Now a final word. We need to say, "It is the Bible and Christ, or nothing." Somebody may say, "It is the Baptist denomination or nothing." But you are wrong, brother, sister. One will soon go into modernism unless he believes it is Christ and the Bible, come Hell or high water. Christ and the Bible—wherever He leads, whatever it teaches!

Somebody wrote about me, "Brother John Rice used to be such a sound Baptist but now he is for so-and-so." Sound Baptist? Maybe so, maybe not. But I've always been for Christ and the Bible, the blood atonement, the virgin birth, the bodily resurrection, Heaven and Hell. If God said it, it is so. I dare you to find any time I have ever wavered on any of that.

You say, "But my friends." Friendship isn't first. It is Christ and the Bible first. You say, "It is the program." Not the program first! Christ and the Bible. "But I'll lose friends." Well, lose them.

America is doomed unless we say, "Friendship or no friendship; democratic party or no party; whether the people lead or don't lead; whether it pays or doesn't pay; whether I get cheaper electricity or not." We had better get back to the American way of life, private ownership of property, paying honest debts, receiving what we deserve, paying what we owe. That is the American way.

And in Christianity it is back to Jesus Christ, the blood, the infallible Bible, and "I will follow it if I lose every friend in the world, and break with everybody." I would rather shake hands and call "brother" any Catholic priest who loves Jesus Christ and believes the Bible than to shake hands with a Baptist who does not believe the Bible!

There is just one safe place and that is saying. "By God's grace I am going to stick right here with the Word."

Closing Prayer:

O God, tonight, do put some iron in the backbones of preachers. O God, put some holy conviction in the hearts of Christians. Help people to say, I will not, God helping me, not with a dime of money, not even with an encouraging word, 1 will not back up infidelity and modernism, the enemies of Jesus Christ. Help us to say, O God, if Jesus says die for Me, I'll die; if He says lose friends, I'll lose them, but I'll stay true to Christ and the Bible. Help us in Jesus' name, Amen.

The Lord Our Righteousness

(Preached Sunday night, May 13, 1956, at Calvary Baptist Church, Wheaton, Ill. Mechanically recorded for THE SWORD OF THE LORD.)

"And I will gather the remnant of my flock out of all countries whither I have driven them, and will bring them again to their folds; and they shall be fruitful and increase. And I will set up shepherds over them which shall feed them: and they shall fear no more, nor be dismayed, neither shall they be lacking, saith the Lord. Behold, the days come, saith the Lord, that I will raise unto David a righteous Branch, and a King shall reign and prosper, and shall execute judgment and justice in the earth. In his days Judah shall be saved, and Israel shall dwell safely: and this is his name whereby he shall be called, THE LORD OUR RIGHTEOUSNESS. Therefore, behold, the days come, saith the Lord, that they shall no more say, The Lord liveth, which brought up the children of Israel out of the land of Egypt; But, The Lord liveth, which brought up and which led the seed of the house of Israel out of the north country, and from all countries whither I had driven them; and they shall dwell in their own land."
—Jer. 23:3-8.

Jeremiah has been prophesying that judgment is coming on the nation Israel. Throughout the book of Jeremiah there is a sob in the throat of the prophet and there are tears in the eyes of the prophet, and Jeremiah is called "the weeping prophet." Nowadays talk of coming calamity is called a jeremiad. That means one who talks like Jeremiah brings a jeremiad, that is, a prophecy of doom.

But in the midst of all these promises of judgment and captivity—the children of Israel led into Babylon, Jerusalem destroyed, the temple torn down—God gives the promise: "I see the day." God said, "I will bring back all my flock from the countries where I have driven them, and I will bring them back to their own land." He said, "I will set shepherds over my people, over my flock, and I will raise a righteous King, the seed of David, a branch of the seed of David." He will be called "THE LORD OUR RIGHTEOUSNESS," the Scripture says.

I. THE RESTORATION OF ALL GOOD THINGS FOR GOD'S PEOPLE

Now this is the promise of the literal restoration of the nation Israel, but also the restoration of things for Christians. Here God calls the people of Israel "my flock," "my sheep," "the sheep of my pasture." But David said for all of us Christians, "The Lord is *my* shepherd." If I ever hear any Jew saying, "Jesus Christ is my shepherd," I will say, "He is mine, too!" Then the Jew will say, "But Abraham is my father." And I will say, "Oh, yes, but I trusted the Lord like faithful Abraham; so I am Abraham's seed, too, according to the promise."

Somebody says, "I'm a Jew." I answer back, "One is not a Jew who is just a Jew outwardly, but one who is a Jew inwardly, and I am of the chosen people, too." And he may say, 'But I am of the true, tame olive tree, the Jews." I answer, "But I am the wild olive branch that was grafted into the same stalk, praise God! And all the promises there are mine too."

If I hear a Jew say, "But I have been circumcised," I will say, "Yes, I have been circumcised in heart," and so one blessed day Jews will be circumcised in heart, too, and then Jews and Gentiles, the middle wall of partition broken down between them, and all God's people, the Jews who have been converted and Gentiles who have been converted. So this is the story of the restoration of Israel, but it is also the picture of a restoration of all things good for Christians and others.

1. Israel to Be Restored to Palestine and God's Favor

Notice first the promise of Israel's restoration. This is a wonderful thing. God has promised to restore Israel. And in this case, God did not say, "I am going to bring a remnant back from Babylon." Though He did that, that is not the point. This is not just the time God sent Moses, and sent the plagues, and all the children of Israel crossed the Red Sea dryshod, and God fed them manna in the wilderness, and brought them into their own land. But He said, "This will be the time when everybody will say, 'Oh, the Lord sent His angels and gathered out Israel from every nation under Heaven where God had carried them." From *all* countries! That means from slave labor camps in Siberia. That means from wherever they work everywhere. Whether there is a Jew in a bank, or whether there is a Jew in a drygoods store having a fire sale, or whether there is a Jew who runs a junk yard, God will gather every Jew alive in the world back to Palestine, and after the rebels are purged out, they will be converted. Here is a wonderful, wonderful promise.

There are many promises about this in the Bible.

God had said, in Genesis 13:14, 15, 'Abraham, look north, east, south, and west, for all the land that thou seest, to thee will I give it and to thy seed forever.' God said, 'I am going to give you this land. So God is going to give the land to Abraham and to his seed. And in the book of Galatians we learn that seed is singular, not plural. Not many seeds, but one seed—Christ. So in Christ's own return God will give the land to Abraham and to Jesus Christ as well as to Jews and Gentiles who love the Lord Jesus Christ. That promise is so often told.

Again God gave the promise to David. "David, the Lord also telleth thee that He will make thee an house." He said, "Your seed after you will inherit the kingdom and he will build the temple, the house for my name, and I will establish the throne of his kingdom forever. And his throne shall be established forever." (See II Samuel 7:10-17, I Chronicles 17:10-15). One day the throne of David will be established forever, and David's seed will sit on that throne again.

Do you remember the promises given in Deuteronomy, chapter 30 to the nation Israel? The Scripture says:

"And it shall come to pass, when all these things are come upon thee, the blessing and the curse, which I have set before thee, and thou shalt call to mind among all the nations, whither the Lord thy God hath driven thee, And shalt return unto the Lord thy God, and shalt obey his voice according to all that I command thee this day, thou and thy children, with all thine heart, and with all thy soul; That then the Lord thy God will turn thy captivity, and have compassion upon thee, and will return," [the Lord will return! That is the personal, literal return of Jesus Christ.] *"and gather thee from all nations, whither the Lord thy God hath scattered thee. If any of thine be driven out unto the outmost parts of heaven, from thence will the Lord thy God gather thee, and from thence will he fetch thee."*

(Notice how complete is that regathering. If there be one single Jew left alive anywhere in the world, God will bring him back. That is not a little partial restoration like a handful of Jews now, unconverted Jews back in Palestine. They don't even have control of all of Jerusalem, now—about two counties or three of Jews in a little part of Palestine now. That is not the restoration God is talking about.):

"And the Lord thy God will bring thee into the land which thy fathers possessed, and thou shalt possess it; and he will do thee good, and multiply thee above thy fathers. And the Lord thy God will circumcise thine heart, and the heart of thy seed, to love the Lord thy God with all thine heart, and with all thy soul, that thou mayest live."—Deut. 30:1-6.

How many times that promise is given! That promise was given to Mary by the angel when Jesus was to come, and the Virgin Mary was told that she should conceive a child and that He should be called the Son of the Highest, then the Angel Gabriel told Mary, "The Lord God shall give unto him the throne of his father David: And he shall reign over the house of Jacob for ever" (Luke 1:32, 33). I don't wonder then, that when Jesus rode into Jerusalem upon a colt, the foal of an ass, they said, "Hosanna to the son of David." One of these days He is coming on a white horse, crowned with many crowns, with the armies of Heaven following Him. And Jesus will restore the Jews.

That promise that He will restore Israel is given also in the words of the Saviour Himself in Matthew 24, beginning with verse 29. Notice carefully how this is dated in God's plan: "Immediately after the tribulation of those days": [When is this coming now? After the tribulation. After the rapture. After the tribulation. After the Antichrist has reigned on earth. Then what?] "shall the sun be darkened, and the moon shall not give her light, and the stars shall fall from heaven, and the powers of the heavens shall be shaken: And then shall appear the sign of the Son of man in heaven: and then shall all the tribes of the earth mourn, and they shall see the Son of man coming in the clouds of heaven with power and great glory." Not for the rapture. Then we will be caught up in the air in a moment to meet the Lord as the lightning flashes from the east to the west. And we will be gone for a honeymoon in Heaven. Not that. But *after that.* After the tribulation, after the Antichrist— now Jesus comes back to reign. "And he shall send his angels with a great sound of a trumpet, and they shall gather together his elect [Who are the chosen people? Who is the specially elected nation? Israel.] from the four winds, from one end of heaven to the other" (Matt. 24:31).

You see, then, that Israel's restoration is promised through all the Bible. No one has a right to wave it aside.

But let us get one more word from Paul the apostle. Paul writes, ". . . Hath God cast away his people? God forbid . . . God hath not cast away his people which he foreknew . . . ." (Rom. 11:1, 2). "No," he said, "a Jew has much to gain every way because God used the Jew to bring the Bible, and from the Jews Christ came. And then he said, "There is coming a time when the blindness which has happened to Israel shall be done away, until the fulness of the Gentiles be come in." Then God is going to graft that broken branch of the tame olive tree back into the tree again. And the Scripture says, ". . . so all Israel shall be saved . . ." (Rom. 11:26). So one of these blessed days God will regather His people, the Jews, and purge out the rebels, and all the unconverted will be saved, and the Lord Jesus Christ will sit on the throne of David, His father.

Jesus had two "fathers," in Bible language. On His mother's side, His ancestor was David. On the divine side, His ancestor was God. He is the Son of God, Son of David. And He will come to reign on David's throne.

In Matthew 25:31, the Scripture says, "When the Son of man shall come in his glory, and all the holy angels with him, then shall he sit upon the throne of his glory." Jesus is coming to reign and to regather the Jews.

Now what is going to be involved in this great restoration? What will be regathered? The Jewish people, for one thing. God who seems to have cast away the Jews, God who has judged the Jews—oh, how they have been judged and punished. But God says He will regather them and comfort them as one whom his mother comforteth. God has told us that He will restore the Jews. It is the nation that He let be scattered into Babylonian captivity, and then He brought back a remnant with Nehemiah and Ezra; the nation of the Jews that were dispersed into all the world in A. D. 70 when Titus, the Roman emperor, destroyed Jerusalem; the Jews, so persecuted that 6 million of them were killed by Hitler in World War II. (Out of 15 million Jews in the world, forty per cent of them were killed by Hitler and the German armies.) But now, thank God, God will restore the nation Israel to favor, and the spiritual blindness will be done away, and they will see their Messiah. The Lord says that in Jerusalem when the Jews are brought back there will be opened in that day a fountain for sin and uncleanness. And they will look on Him whom they pierced and they will say, "What are these wounds in thy hands?" And He will say, "I was wounded in the house of my friends." The Jews then will mourn, every family apart, as they repent of their sins, and a nation shall be born in a day. A wonderful time!

So Jews will be themselves restored to favor as a nation.

Another thing involved is the land, the land of Palestine, that little rocky land that has been the battlefield of the nations, that little connecting link between Europe and Asia and Africa, across which the armies of Babylon and Media-Persia, and Rome, and before that the armies of Egypt, and now since that, the armies of two world wars, and not only that, but across that same peninsula, across those same mountains and rivers and wonders, one day will come again the battles of the kings of the east and then the Battle of Armageddon. The battleground of the world is Palestine in some sense. But, thank God, the land is promised as the chosen land of God. God said about Jerusalem, "I have placed my name there perpetually." And God said, "Abraham, walk through this land of Canaan. I have given it to you for an everlasting possession." One day, thank God, that land will be restored to favor. It is a dry land now, and the trees are mostly gone. They are replanting some trees in Israel and planting orange groves, and they are digging some oil wells, and they are trying to restore its economy, though it is largely kept up by gifts from Jews in America. But one time, bless God, the sandy desert will be no more. The cedars in Lebanon will grow again, the giant trees it once had, and the grapes of Eshcol and the pomegranates and the olive yards and the vineyards will make it a land flowing with milk and honey again in the favor of God. God will restore the land and the people to the land.

Not only so, but the people of Israel will be brought back and converted, the Scripture says. They will be turned in heart and then they will be circumcised in heart, in the hearts of their seed, to love the Lord their God. And He said, "I will take out the stony heart and put a heart of flesh within you and you will serve God."

Another thing restored there will be the kingdom of David. There was the throne. A man after God's own heart sat on it. The sweet singer of Israel who wrote the twenty-third Psalm, the thirty-seventh, the thirty-fourth, the hundred and third—the sweet singer, David, had built the throne. And God loved it. One day God will put a Son of David on that throne; a branch will grow out of his root, a branch of David. This sprout comes off of the old stump where the tree is cut down and the Davidic dynasty cut off from remembrance, a sprout comes up and the tree grows again and the kingdom of David is re-established with Jesus Christ sitting on the throne. All this is involved in the restoration that is coming to Israel.

2. The Good Things Lost Will Be Restored for God's Children

Now then, the lost will be restored! Oh, that is a wonderful theme, and that takes in all of us and we can together thank God for it, that the lost will be restored. First of all, Israel will be restored to favor and that is wonderful. Wouldn't it be a sad thing for all the saints of God who have read about David and Abraham and Elijah and all the saints of God, read about Moses (the Ten Commandments came through the Jews)—wouldn't it be a pitiful thing if we had a Heaven with no Jews in it? Jerusalem! Why, even Heaven is named after Jerusalem. It is called the New Jerusalem. A Heaven and no Jewish nation and psalms, and prophets and traditions and teachings? Thank God, Israel is restored, that which was a castaway. Israel is like a wife who played the harlot and ran after other men, and God said, "But I have loved you and I will take you back again." A wife restored to favor—that is Israel. That will be wonderful, won't it?

But that isn't all. The ground will be restored to Israel and that will be wonderful. You know, this ground brings forth thorns and thistles. If anybody here ever worked at growing crops, ever lived on a farm, ever worked in a vineyard, you will know there is a need for this. You cannot enjoy a yard for the mosquitoes that come to bite and torment you. You cannot have a lawn but what you have to dig out the dandelions. You cannot have a garden without having chickens scratch it up, or rabbits or squirrels eat off the tops of the vegetables. You have rust if it is wheat, or the smut, or crow poison if it is corn, or you have this or that or the other. Or you have drought and thorns, pests and disease. You have to spray your apple trees or the worms will get them. There is a curse on the earth. All the storms, all the hurricanes, and the briars! You cannot have a rose without thorns, or a beautiful animal but it is afraid of mankind.

There is an enmity between man and nature. There is an enmity between man and the sea, between man and the ground. God said, "Cursed is the ground for thy sake . . . Thorns also and thistles shall it bring forth to thee . . ." (Gen. 3:17, 18). But, blessed be God, that which was lost will be restored. We are going to have a new Garden of Eden. One of these days the desert shall blossom as a rose and bring forth abundantly, and in the deserts shall springs of water spring up. It will be a good thing, bless God, with no more desert; a good thing, bless God, with no more drought; a good thing, with no more fields taken over by Russian thistle; a good thing when the pests will be no more. You won't have to spray to kill disease germs and to kill bugs and worms. We have elm trees in our yards here in Wheaton and in Glen Ellyn, and if we didn't go together and spray them out, the fungus would take over our trees, and they would soon die with Dutch elm disease. A few years ago all the chestnut trees died in America. Now you cannot find a native chestnut tree anywhere in this country. All over America they have been killed by a plague that we couldn't stop. But, bless God, one of these days chestnut trees will grow again. One of these blessed days the curse on the ground will be removed. One of these days every seed you plant will grow like Jack-and-the-bean-stalk's beans did! It will even be better than Perry's Seed Catalog pictures it! (Now you city slickers don't know about that. If you never did get a seed catalog down in the springtime and think about what you would plant—Early Breakfast radishes, they called them; and Country Gentleman sweet corn; and Beefsteak tomatoes; then you don't know about that.) But one day the frustration of having the ground accursed and the plant life accursed and every animal an enemy, and all the unseen insect world and microbe world at enmity with mankind and set to kill, will be done away with.

And that means also the curse on animals will be taken away. Animals will be restored. The lion shall eat straw like an ox. The lion and the lamb shall lie down together and a little child shall play on the cockatrice's den. "And they shall not hurt nor destroy in all my holy mountain: for the earth shall be full of the knowledge of the Lord, as the waters cover the sea," says the Scripture (Isa. 11:9). There will be a restored Garden of Eden.

It was too bad the day that God had to send an angel with a flaming sword and say, "Adam, you've sinned. Eve, you've sinned. I have to drive you out, for you would eat of the tree of life and live forever in sin, live forever away from God, and go on your bold way in sin." So with a flaming sword the angel of God drove them out and barred the gates of Eden. The Garden of Eden grew up in brush and weeds, I suppose, and God removed it from the earth. One day there will be a paradise of God again and the birds will sing sweetly, the mosquitoes won't bite. There will be no thorns on the roses, no plague and curse on the earth. Then what about the animals? Thank God, in that sweet time, with land restored, animals will be the friends of men and the favored companions of men. We will have this new earth God is going to make. God will restore Israel, and God will restore the ground, and God will restore the balance of a perfect creation one of these days.

3. Our Bodies Will Be Restored to Youth and Health

And that isn't all! God will restore our bodies.

I am not just saying this is a simile. I am not just drawing some illustrations. I mean that *I* have a part! Praise God, when God brings back the Jews . . . Don't you remember He said in Ephesians that God has broken down the middle wall of partition and made both one. We were strangers and foreigners but now we are made nigh by the blood of Jesus Christ. And I am as good a Jew then as David. I am just as good a Jew as the twelve apostles. I may not be as good a man but I am as good a Jew because I am circumcised in heart, and the seed of Abraham by faith, and so God takes me and the middle wall is all taken down. When Jesus died on the cross and the earthquake came and the veil of the temple was rent from the top to the bottom . . . Yonder were two courts. Between the court of the Levites and the court of the Gentiles there was a stone wall. And the veil of the temple was torn from the top to the bottom and ripped open so that there was no more barrier between man and God. Anybody who will can walk into the very Holy of Holies to face God—nothing between! And that same day, the middle wall of partition between the court of the Gentiles and the court of the Levites was broken down, and Gentiles may not only go into the temple court, but into the place of the Levites and priests. We are free! Thank God, the middle wall of partition is broken down and so we can come boldly to the throne of grace.

So we are going to have resurrection bodies, in a moment, in the twinkling of an eye.

I feel this, I guess, a good deal more than others. I'll have to make a confession. I never expected to grow old. Even yet if I were very sensible I would probably look around on other men sixty years old, and I would say, "Well, some of these days after I get about eighty, I will be like these other men sixty years old." But I don't really believe it. I guess God will make me know it some day. I still don't see any reason why I shouldn't ride horseback, or why I shouldn't play tennis, or why I shouldn't run, or play baseball, or do work. If I get down to Bill's for the work week and somebody needs to lift 600 pounds and put up big beams in the roof, I won't see why I'm not to do it. But all the time I find that I go up the stairs a little slower than I used to, and that if I jump around too much my knees are a little stiffer than they used to be, and I someway feel, "How sad, how sad that this body is getting stiff," because I had such a strong body, so active and strong and vigorous. But one day I will have my youth again. One day "the eyes of the blind shall be opened, the ears of the deaf shall be unstopped, and the lame man shall leap as an hart, and the tongue of the dumb shall sing." So that which is gone will be restored. Won't that be good! Anybody here getting blind? Well, you will see well one of these days! I just want to see Bob Main prancing around then on both legs. I want to see him that time, bless God, when the youth is restored and when that which we've lost (sometimes through no fault of ours, sometimes through the ravages of the years) will be restored.

There is a little poem once popular; it is a little old-fashioned now, which says:

Backward, turn backward, O Time, in your flight,
And make me a child again just for tonight.

That never comes now. But one day it will come, and youth will be restored, and lost vision, the lost enthusiasm, lost appetite, and lost capacity to eat—you can run all night and never want to go to bed—bless God, that will be restored. The lost things will be restored when Israel is restored. Won't that be a good thing? Amen! That time will come.

Not only will our bodies be restored and our natures perfected, but oh the sin question! We have lost so much.

I was raised in rather a protected way. It is surprising considering that I lived in the wild West Texas country and I had no mother, but I was a preacher's boy. I was converted when I was nine years old. I am shocked and surprised to find all the time that youngsters in their early teens know more about the things of the world than I did. They know more about sex than I knew when I was married. I look back on those days and my face was the face of a youngster, of a youth. And when I was a preacher, my wife used to say, "Better not shave today. They think you are so young." I used to get out and rustle up some old run-down church and have revival services and get people revived and get people saved, and have a wonderful time. Then they would say, "We ought to buckle down and get to business. We ought to call a pastor." Some of the young people would say, "Let's call Brother Rice."

They would say, "No, he's too young. We need an older man for a pastor." So they would call somebody else as pastor and I would go pull another old run-down place together and they would call some older man, someone more mature. But oh, bless God for the glory of youth! It will be restored one day.

And if anybody thinks that I have a good deal of push and get-up, you ought to have seen me back thirty years ago. Miss Viola thinks I work her pretty hard now till six o'clock in the evening when other people work till five, but she and Miss Fairy and Miss Lola would tell you that it used to be till one o'clock in the morning a good many times in the old days. I am just saying that one day the drive and enthusiasm and innocency and freshness and dew of youth will be restored again!

4. Innocence Will Be Restored to God's People

You know, sin is a terrible thing. And I suppose everybody who ever sinned—oh, we think of what might have been.

Of all sad words of tongue and pen,
The saddest are these: "It might have been."

Oh, it might have been! And men look back on wasted youth and wish they had it to live over again.

I remember a drunkard who knelt with me in the Capital Hotel in Amarillo, Texas, and prayed. He had tried to commit suicide. His wife had already left him because of his sin. He was a wastrel, a drunken wretch, profligate with his money and in his life! He knelt down to pray and he said, "O God, make me a good boy like my mamma wanted me to be!" He was sad because his goodness and the freshness of youth was gone. "Oh, I've made such a mistake. I wish I had it to do over," he thought. Well, bless God, one day God will restore it.

Isn't it a wonderful thing that God can undo the past and make it clean again?

A man lay on the hospital bed who had wasted his life in sin. Now his body was broken and the doctors did all they could. A friend came and hovered around and said, "What can I bring you? Anything I can get you?"

"No, there is nothing you can do."

"Let me bring you a good book to read."

"No, thank you. I don't care."

"Well, then, may I bring you some ice cream?"

"No, no."

"I'll bring a basket of fruit. What can I do? Is there anything I can do for you? Would you like some flowers?"

"Oh, no, no!" the man said, the man on the hospital bed, an old man. He had gone in sin, his body broken down in sin.

The man said, "What can I do?"

And then the sick man said this: "There is nothing you can do. There is nothing *anybody* can do. Oh, God, if there were only somebody who could *undo!*"

Well, thanks be to God, one day Israel, the prodigal, will be brought back, the harlot wife will be restored, the desert place will be made springs of water, the eyes of the blind will be opened, the ears of the deaf will be unstopped, the converted harlot will be pure again as she once was, the saved drunkard will be sober again, the penitent thief will be honest again. And, blessed be God, the wicked and vile will again be pure and good. Aren't you glad that those who put their trust in Jesus will have a great time of restoration when the bad things will be made good and the things that we failed in will be restored. Thank God, the Scripture says He will restore the years that the locusts have eaten.

That is what the prodigal boy thought about when his money was all gone. He said, "I have played the fool. I have wasted my substance in riotous living." And the older brother said he had wasted it with harlots. Then in a hog pen he came to himself. He got his senses about him and he said, "I will arise and go to my father."

He is sobbing as he goes home. What does he want? "O God, I wish I was back as a child. If Dad would let me come back, if I can just listen to my mother and my dad, and eat at home, and be content—I wish he would restore it."

Thank God, it was restored! His father saw him a great way off and ran and fell on his neck and kissed him. And the boy started to say, "Father, I have sinned. I am not fit to be your boy."

But the father interrupted him and said, "Bring the best robe and put on him. And bring shoes for his feet, and bring a ring for his finger! Kill the fatted calf and call the neighbors to come in for supper! My boy was dead and is alive again!"

Oh, the wasted years are undone, wiped out, paid off and forgotten, and the boy is back home again. "My son was dead and is alive again. He was lost and is found."

Yes, there is coming a time when the lost will be found, when the dead will be made alive, when the wasted will be restored, when the drought will be over, when the frown and the disfavor of God will be removed and there will be a loving smile on the face of God again. Well, that is what the boy meant. When Jesus was crucified, that was what that boy, man, thief on the cross meant when he looked over at Jesus and saw over his head, "This is the King of the Jews." He saw by faith the restoration of Israel and David's, kingdom, and he said, "If I had a chance in a good government, in a good land, and with Jesus to help me! Lord Jesus, when you come to your kingdom remember me."

Jesus answered, "I won't wait until the kingdom. Even now, today shalt thou be with me in paradise." And he who was a thief is made a saint. And he who was too sorry and wicked to live on earth in society was made fit for the angels of God, and God Almighty's society, and taken home to Heaven. Oh, the lost restored! Won't that be good! When Israel is restored, much else will be restored, too, thank God!

As I preached in Dallas, Texas, in the Fry Furniture Building one day a sad woman sat near the front and quietly wiped away the tears. Her face was marked. The unhappiness, the lines, the frustration, the sensualness, the grossness that goes with sin marks a woman's face. She looked very sad, as well she might. At the close she didn't come forward. I gave the invitation, and I said, "Come on."

She said, "Preacher, don't torment me. I can't come. Please. There's no use."

"Oh, yes, you *can* come."

"No, I can't. There is no use making me more miserable. There is nothing I can do about it. Please let me alone."

I said, "Yes, you can come."

"No," she said, "I can't."

I asked, "Why not?"

"Because," and she broke out into sobbing again, "I can't forget what I have done! I can't forget what I've done!"

I turned to the tenth chapter of Hebrews and told her how this man by one offering hath sanctified forever them that are his. I read that to her, then I showed her where the Scriptures said, after these things "there remaineth no more sacrifice for sins" (Heb. 10:26). And the Scripture which says, "And their sins and iniquities will I remember no more" (Heb. 10:17).

I said, "Don't you see, God says He won't even remember them anymore! They are blotted out. They are forgotten. And God won't ever remember them. Don't you think He can help *you* forget?"

How glad she was to find that God would blot them out and even forget them, and never even remember them any more. And how gladly she came to trust the Lord Jesus! Thank God, a restoration is coming to all of us who trust in the Lord Jesus.

II. THE LORD OUR RIGHTEOUSNESS

But I come to another word here and that is the one who is sitting on the throne of David. King of kings, He shall reign in righteousness and judgment. Turn back to that wonderful passage in Jeremiah 23, and read it again. Look at it now in verses 5 and 6: "Behold, the days come, saith the Lord, that I will raise unto David a righteous Branch, and a King shall reign and prosper, and shall execute judgment and justice in the earth. In his days Judah shall be saved, and Israel shall dwell safely (But what is his name? What is His name? Oh, the names of Jesus in the Bible!) : and this is his name whereby he shall be called, THE LORD OUR RIGHTEOUSNESS."

There are many beautiful names of Jesus. He is the bright and morning star. He is the lion of the tribe of Judah. He is the Alpha and Omega, the beginning and the end, which means the first and last letters of the Greek alphabet. What else is He called? The Son of man, the Son of Abraham, the Son of David, the Son of God. Oh, wonderful! But here is the name for us today: ". . . this is his name whereby he shall be called, THE LORD OUR RIGHTEOUSNESS."

1. Jesus Is the Only Truly Righteous One

In the first place, Jesus is righteous. He is *THE* righteous One. He is the only purely righteous one this world ever saw. I thank God, He is righteous. He is as righteous as God the Father. He is the express image of His person. He is one with the Father. He is God's agent in creation. He is God's agent in judgment. God has committed all judgment to the Son. He is God's agent in the writing of the book, the Bible, for the Bible is the word of Christ. "Let the word of Christ dwell in you richly . . ." (Col. 3:16). Oh, the Son, Jesus! He is sinless and perfect. Is anybody looking for goodness?

You remember a Greek philosopher, Diogenes, went through the streets of Athens with a lighted lantern day and night. People asked, "What is it? What are you seeking, Diogenes?"

He said, "To find an honest man."

He never seemed to find him an honest man.

You look about for good men but there are no good men, except by human standards that are very limited, and they fail. Some pressure comes and they fail. You talk about some honest, trustworthy man, "a man who is as good as his bond." Every man tells the truth up to a certain point. The point differs with different men. There is always a point where a man doesn't tell the truth, partly because he doesn't even see the truth, and because it would get him in trouble if he did, or go against his pride. Except by a limited human concept, there are no honest men. But put it up by the side of God and there are only men who are sinners.

This is sad. But there are no pure women except by a limited human concept. There are women who haven't played the harlot There are women who are nice, good women by every human standard. But the Bible says, "There is no difference: For all have sinned, and come short of the glory of God" (Rom. 3:23). So in God's sight there are no pure women, there are no honest men.

In God's sight there are no innocent babies. Brother Fast, that infant of yours is not innocent. She is not intentionally guilty now, but by the time she is three weeks old, if you take and hold her head like you want it held, she will raise Ned and kick and scream and want her own way. The Bible says, ". . . they go astray as soon as they be born, speaking lies." Even a little baby lies. In the middle of the night he howls and says, "My tummy hurts. Hurry! Help me out!" You pick him up and it wasn't his stomach at all. He was lying. He just wanted you to hold him, that is all! I know, because six of them lied to me. Isn't that right, Mrs. Rice? There are not any innocent babies except in a limited concept, a human concept. There are no pure women.

There are no good men till you come to Jesus Christ. Thank God, He is innocent and pure and good. Of Him the dying thief could say, ". . . this man hath done nothing amiss" (Luke 23:41). Only this one could say, "Ye are from beneath: I am from above" (John 8:23). Only this one could say, "Which of you convinceth me of sin? . . ." (John 8:46). I don't dare ask anybody to show me where I have ever done wrong. I don't dare. Miss Viola is always showing me, my wife is always showing me, my children are always showing me. My sons-in-law try but I keep pretty well ahead of them. I don't let them catch up on me so much. But I am just saying that only Jesus Christ can ever look the world in the face and say, "Who can convince me of sin?" But now He is the righteous one. So it is right to say that it is not only that He is the *most* righteous, it is not only that He is one who is righteous, but Jesus is the *only* righteous man who ever walked the earth! Son of man, Son of God, Son of Abraham, Son of David, and Son of mankind. He is the second Adam. The first Adam—a sinner. The second Adam —pure and sinless. Thanks be to God!

The first baby ever born in this world was Cain, a murderer. He didn't grow up in a pool hall. He didn't have a bad environment. There wasn't anybody he could lay it on. It was built-in wickedness. Every child ever born has the same wickedness but the innocent, blameless Son of God. He is the righteous one, bless God.

2. Christ, the Righteousness of God, Took My Place, Paid My Debt

And not only that, He is not only the righteous one, but He is our substitute. Do you need somebody to pay for sin? Jesus Christ can pay for sin, and nobody else can. Nobody else is fit to. Thank God, Jesus Christ paid for sins. One day God let them nail Jesus to a cross and He who knew no sin became sin for us that we might become the righteousness of God in Him. Oh, one day God took all the holiness of Heaven, all the innocence, all the purity, all the goodness, all the riches, all of it concentrated in Jesus Christ, the express image of the Father Himself, and God had Him nailed to a cross. The curse of mankind was on Him for, "Cursed is every one that hangeth on a tree" (Gal. 3: 13). God turned His face away from Him. The earth trembled and shook and the sky was as black as sackcloth of hair, and the veil in the temple was rent in twain, and the graves opened and people came out after His resurrection. God let Jesus, the innocent, die for the guilty. Jesus became my substitute. That means then that Jesus is now imputed my righteousness. That is, his righteousness is charged to my account.

If somebody knocks at my door and asks, "What is in this house? Is it sin? Is it ruin? Is it impending judgment? Is it that which calls down the wrath of God? What is in this house?"

I answer back, "In this house is all the righteousness and holiness and purity and goodness of God, for the Son dwells in here and He has paid my debt." And, thank God, even a holy God cannot charge anything else up because that has been paid. The whole debt has been paid. It is imputed to me.

God counted Jesus a sinner when He was not a sinner, so now God has a right to count me righteous when I am not righteous. That is imputed righteousness. That is the reason that Psalm 32, as it is quoted over here in Romans 4 . . . What about this righteousness? The Lord said, in talking about Abraham as our example, "How about this righteousness? Was it just for the Jews only or was it for us also?" Now listen to it: "For what saith the scripture? Abraham believed God, and it was counted unto him for righteousness. Now to him that worketh is the reward not reckoned of grace, but of debt. [If you work for it—but I didn't work for it. I *couldn't* work for it. I couldn't pay it. I got it free!] But to him that worketh not [that is me], but believeth on him that justifieth the ungodly . . . ."

[Justifies what kind of people? Ungodly! A fellow doesn't work and isn't godly, and yet he gets justified and counted just. Do you know what it means to be counted just? That doesn't mean that you are pardoned after you sin. It means you are tried and found not guilty! God looks on me and says, "Well, there is nothing wrong with him in the world. Everything that was ever wrong is fixed. It is all paid. It is all clear. He has paid the last penny. Jesus paid it for me. God counts it settled. So then even as David described it, the blessedness of the man unto whom God imputeth righteousness without works. That is a substitute righteousness. Jesus paid His righteousness to take the place of my sin. So He is my substitute.]

"But to him that worketh not, but believeth on him that justifieth the ungodly, his faith is counted for righteousness. Even as David also describeth the blessedness of the man, unto whom God imputeth righteousness without works, Saying, Blessed are they whose iniquities are forgiven, and whose sins are covered. Blessed is the man to whom the Lord will not impute sin" (Rom. 4:3-8). So we can say, "Thank God, Jesus Christ has imputed His righteousness to me."

Not only is Jesus Christ, the Son, *imputed* as my righteousness. The Lord our Righteousness is His name.

But another blessed truth: He is my imparted righteousness. Not only does God charge up the righteousness to me, but God is an honest God and God says, "Well, if I am going to count John Rice righteous I sure have a job on my hands, because now I have to make him righteous." God says, "I am honest and square and if I am going to count John Rice righteous and put him down in the records, and have it all through the ages that John Rice is counted righteous, I sure have a job on my hands because I am going to make him what I claim him to be."

So God puts His Spirit within me. And I became a partaker of the divine nature and Christ is in me, the hope of glory. And I begin to be like Him. Paul said, "I have not already attained. I am not yet perfect. But I press toward the mark for the prize of the high calling of God in Christ Jesus." One of these days the race will be ended and all of Paul's striving will be over. Then in a moment he will be made as pure and good as he had longed to be. One of these days in a moment the voice of the archangel and the trump of God shall sound and the dead in Christ shall rise, and we wait for His Son from Heaven who shall change our vile bodies like unto His glorious body. Then, thank God, I, who am already counted righteous in Heaven, will suddenly be completely righteous. And God has made me then what He claimed me to be and reckoned me to be before.

3. Christ Thus Becomes the Believer's Salvation

Now read that story again back here in Jeremiah 23. What is the wonderful name? ". . . and this is his name whereby he shall be called, THE LORD OUR RIGHT-

EOUSNESS." Jesus Christ *my* righteousness.

I come to say two things now about it. First of all, if the Lord is my righteousness, that fixes my salvation. There is not anything better than that!

Somebody says, "I have the church."

I have Jesus!

"I have baptism," you say.

I have Jesus Christ, the righteousness of God.

You say, "But I have been confirmed."

Yes, but I have Jesus Christ, the righteousness of God.

Somebody says, "I have all of life well lived."

I have the absolute perfection of Jesus Christ. He is in me! I have Him. Any boat I am in has perfect righteousness in it. Any house I live in has perfect righteousness in it. Any suit of clothes I wear has perfect righteousness in it. Brother, I cannot be separated from it. Thanks be unto God, I am persuaded that neither life, nor death, nor principalities, nor powers, nor things present, nor things to come, nor height, nor depth, nor any other creature shall be able to separate us from the love of God which is in Jesus Christ our Lord. I have Christ my righteousness, and He is making me righteous. The Devil cannot get me.

"Who is he that condemneth? It is Christ that died, yea rather, that is risen again . . ." (Rom. 8:34). ". . . If God be for us, who can be against us?" (Rom. 8:31). You see, my salvation is sure.

Listen! Not only is my salvation sure, but my eternal safety is sure

Somebody says, "But, Brother Rice, suppose you do wrong?"

Well, it isn't supposition—it is a certainty! But my debt is paid!

Somebody says, "But, Brother Rice, do you suppose you could commit the unpardonable sin?"

How could I when my sins are already pardoned? All my sins are already pardoned. Not going to be pardoned when I die—I am pardoned now! My sins are already blotted out! "Beloved, now are we the sons of God, and it doth not yet appear what we shall be . . ." (I John 3:2). "He that believeth on him is not condemned . . ." (John 3:18). You see, I am already saved, already justified, already not condemned. Sin is already blotted out.

You say, "But suppose you do wrong?"

Well, if I do wrong, I am God's child. He may whip me for it, and I will suffer for it, but, thank God, my salvation is on the basis of Jesus Christ, THE LORD OUR RIGHTEOUSNESS.

'I bear record about the Jews. This is where they have gone wrong,' Paul said. "For I bear them record that they have a zeal of God, but not according to knowledge. For they being ignorant of God's righteousness, and going about to establish their own righteousness, have not submitted themselves unto the righteousness of God" (Rom. 10:2, 3). That is their trouble. They had their own way of righteousness. "For Christ is the end of the law for righteousness to every one that believeth" (Rom. 10:4).

Have you personally put your

trust in Jesus Christ? The Ten Commandments, every law of God ever made—is all filled. All settled! Praise the Lord!

Somebody says, "I have worked for years." Some Jews said, "I have brought my tithes, kept the passover, I was circumcised the eighth day, I have kept the Jewish sabbath, and brought all the sacrifices."

Yes, I know. But all that is now settled in a moment. I have Jesus Christ, THE LORD OUR RIGHTEOUSNESS.

Listen! I have the high priest myself! I have the Lamb of God, the sacrifice! I have everything, everything in the heart, when I have Jesus. I have Jesus!

4. This Is My Assurance of Salvation

How am I going to have assurance? How will I know I am saved?

Brother, when you have Jesus, that settles the whole business. "And this is the record, that God hath given to us eternal life, [not sold it to us—given it to us!] and this life is in his Son. He that hath the Son hath life; and he that hath not the Son of God hath not life. These things have I written unto you that believe on the name of the Son of God; *that ye may know* that ye have eternal life, and that ye may believe on the name of the Son of God" (I John 5:11-13). All of it is yours when you have Jesus. You have the whole business.

How many have Him? How many say, "Thanks be to God, He is THE LORD MY RIGHTEOUSNESS, my redemption, my salvation, my sanctification, my eternal hope of glory—everything! And I have Him tonight." Praise the Lord! How many can say, "I have Him"? He is THE LORD OUR RIGHTEOUSNESS.

Let's say that word together: "... and this is his name whereby he shall be called, THE LORD OUR RIGHTEOUSNESS." My righteousness! My Jesus! My Saviour, my dear Saviour.

Our Heavenly Father, come in power today. Oh come now. If there be anybody not sure of salvation, bring them tonight to know it for sure, and be saved. In Jesus' name.

94

Father, Mother, Home, and Heaven

God's Plan for the Christian Home

(Preached at the Sword of the Lord Conference on Revival and Soul Winning at Toccoa, Georgia, July, 1957)

"And Joshua gathered all the tribes of Israel to Shechem, and called for the elders of Israel, and for their heads, and for their judges, and for their officers; and they presented themselves before God."

"Now therefore fear the Lord, and serve him in sincerity and in truth: and put away the gods which your fathers served on the other side of the flood, and in Egypt; and serve ye the Lord. And if it seem evil unto you to serve the Lord, choose you this day whom ye will serve; whether the gods which your fathers served that were on the other side of the flood [the flood of Jordan before they came into Canaan], or the gods of the Amorites, in whose land ye dwell: but as for me and my house, we will serve the Lord."
—Joshua 24:1, 14, 15.

Joshua said, "Choose you this day whom ye will serve . . . but as for me and my house, we will serve the Lord." Those are wonderful, noble words. Here is a man of God and here is the secret of a man's life, the secret of a home, and in this case, the secret that involved the whole nation. As long as these elders lived who overlived Joshua and they served the Lord with their families, that long Israel stayed true. "As for me and my house, we will serve the Lord."

Now the Bible has the plan for a Christian home. The Bible is the blueprint for everything good and happy. It is never out of date. If you want to know about doctrine, you find it in the Bible. About methods—it is in the Bible. Where a moral or righteous principle or spiritual principle is involved, the Bible has the answer. It tells how to have a Christian family, how to have a happy home life. And it always works.

Here this morning we have Christian people, preachers and Christian workers, and I want to talk about the Christian family. First, consider that the family is a divine institution. In fact, the only thing that Adam and Eve brought with them out of the Garden of Eden was the family, the home. They were married in the Garden of Eden. Marriage is a sacred and beautiful thing, and God is in it. God Himself presented Adam and Eve to each other and performed the first wedding ceremony. Marriage is divine. It is older than church or state, and more important.

God's Plan for Husband and Father

We begin with the man, the head of the home, because that is where God began.

Man Is the Center of a Christian Home

I know we have mottoes on our walls which say, "What is home without a mother." And thank God for Christian mothers. I think I have more reason to thank God for a good wife and a good mother and good women folks than nearly anybody. Before I was six years old my beloved mother had talked to me about the Lord. And when she died before I was six, she made me and others in the family promise to meet her in Heaven. My godly mother gave me to God when I was born and begged God to make me a preacher. I can never get away from the influence of those five and a half short years that I knew my dear mother.

Thank God for a noble Christian wife. She hasn't held me back in my ministry, and has not said, "Don't go. Take it easy. Make more money. Stay here with the children." I have six noble Christian daughters. And I have the help of many Christian women. Three women have worked with me for more than twenty years. Some of the people who love me and pray for me everyday and stand faithfully for what I stand for are godly Christian women.

But we had as well face the facts. You cannot have a really Christian home without a Christian husband and father. That is God's plan. All over America there are good women, noble, Christian women who have married unsaved men and now they struggle along and try to raise their children for God, try to have thanks at the table, try to read the Bible and pray. They try to have a Christian home with a husband who is not saved. And they have found out, with bitter heartache through the years, that it is almost impossible to have more than an outward semblance of a Christian home when the husband and father is not himself a very active leader in that home.

It was not Mrs. Joshua who said, "I'll serve the Lord and see that the old man serves the Lord. You watch me make him hop." But Joshua said, "I'll see to this. As for me and my house, we will serve the Lord."

I say, "Wait a minute, Joshua. You are an old man past eighty. You have boys who are grandfathers. Are you going to take responsibility for all your boys, your sons and sons-in-law, the grandchildren, and maybe some great-grandchildren, and all the servants?"

Joshua answers, "Mind your business, John, and I will mind mine. You see after your family, and I will see after mine. As for me and my house, we will serve the Lord."

The first message about a Christian family has to be to men. God depends on men to lead church, state and home. God intends you men to say, "By God's grace I will see that my home is a Christian home." How blessed it is when a woman does not have to struggle along alone and carry on slender shoulders the weight that was never meant for her. How blessed when God's man takes the place God has for him and makes the home a little picture of Heaven. How sweet home is when God is in it!

Many times when I have preached on the home in great city-wide campaigns, and I have asked the people to sing "Home Sweet Home," they did not know the words. These days the family is scattered. We don't get the whole family together. If they are not eating downtown where they work, they are eating out in night clubs or restaurants or picnic grounds or somewhere else. Since I am away so much, perhaps my home seems dearer to me and stirs my affections more. I am a stranger and a wanderer on the earth. I am an evangelist, and everybody knows that an evangelist is nobody. He is kind of a racketeer, "just out for the money" —you have heard that. An evangelist does not do much Bible preaching; he just strings some deathbed tales together and tear-jerkers, etc., and rakes in a few children and all the shekels he can, and leaves town tomorrow. And if some drunkard is saved, he won't last two weeks, because the preacher was just an evangelist.

You have heard about evangelists, haven't you? Well, I am just an evangelist—no money laid by, no estate, nobody much to take my part. When I come to a new place, everybody looks at me like a calf looking at a new gate and says, "I'll bet he has some twist to that." By the time I am there two or three weeks and God begins to move and drunkards are converted and made sober, and harlots made pure, and infidels made into saints of God, people begin to say, "We need you. Stay longer."

But I have to bid them good-by and many I never see again. It is always good-by for me. I will be glad when it is not always good-by, but "hello"—hello permanently. How sweet it is to get home for some time!

So I know about a home a little more perhaps, and my heart is more stirred with the thought of it. You who are at home so much may be tired of it, and wish you could eat out in big hotels like some other people, and travel on planes, etc. But how sweet it is when we remember that home is a little picture of Heaven, and the relation of husband and wife is a picture of the relation of

Christ and His Church. And the relation of little children to their father is like the relation of Christians to their Heavenly Father. So home ought to be very sweet.

But you have to start with a man.

Man Is in the Image of God and of Christ

You men, sit up straight. Put your feet flat on the floor. You are somebody, not just a forked stick with pants on. You are somebody. Man is made in the image of God. You say, "But I think everybody is—men, women and children." Yes, in a general sense. But men are made in the image of God in a very particular sense. First Corinthians 11:7 says man ought to cut his hair, ought not to pray with his head covered, forasmuch as he is made in the image of God. Women are the image and glory of the man, but the man is made in the image of God, the Scripture says. So a man represents God.

In the first place, no man ought ever to marry unless he says, "I must remember that husbands are to love their wives as Christ loved the Church and gave Himself for it. I am to require of my wife that she obey me as if I were the Lord." That is very serious. So a man better say, "I am somebody. God help me to walk straight. I have a responsibility. I picture Jesus Christ to my wife."

Now some woman may say, "My husband isn't like Jesus." I know, but you married him and God is going to hold you to account. "Wives, be in subjection to your husbands as unto the Lord," the Scripture says. A man in the home is a picture of God the Father. Little children come along and have hero worship. I thank God for something wonderful that was built into my character by my old southern father, and for the hero worship I had for him. My dad was the smartest man in the world, I thought. After I was grown, and was a football tackle, and a broncobuster, and was in the United States Army, and all that, my dad could handle me. The truth is, he had a bluff on me. That is all. My dad was somebody, a real man. And I believed in my dad with that hero worship that is proper and natural for little children toward their father.

Jesus said when you pray say, "Our Father which art in Heaven." The best picture little children ever have of God is their own father, if he be a godly man. Oh, men, you had better watch! God intended for you to take that responsibility.

I wanted my first baby to be a boy, then grow up to be a quarterback at Baylor University, then a preacher, an evangelist. So I ordered a boy! But they were all out of boys and sent me a girl! Then I ordered another boy, but they were still out of boys and sent me another girl! I kept on ordering boys until I had a house full of girls. I used to be partial to boys, but I know when I am licked! I am now partial to girls! When the first baby was born, I sent telegrams to all the kinfolk. When the other girls were born, I sent a post card when I got around to it!

But when the first baby was born I thought, "That beautiful little thing!" You will forgive me—I still think so. There never was a baby as pretty. When they laid that little 6¾ pounds baby in my arms, suddenly I think I became a grown man. I began to feel, "O God, a little body to feed and clothe!" I guess if I had known what I know now—all the nylon stockings, all the piano lessons, all the college tuition, all the church weddings—I would have fainted instead! But I said, "A little body to feed and clothe! A little mind to train for God and Heaven, and an immortal soul for Heaven or Hell!" I thought, "O God, help me to walk straight!" I think I got to be a grown man the day they put that baby girl in my arms.

Listen, a man is somebody! You are not going to have a Christian home until some man says, "By God's grace, I will say like Joshua, 'I will serve the Lord and I will lead my family for God.'" If it is right for Joshua, it is right for John Rice. If it is right for Joshua, it is right for Dr. Robert G. Lee. If it is right for Joshua, it is right for Jack Hyles, and right for the rest of you. Every man here ought to say, "By God's grace I will live for Jesus and take my family along with me." Thank God, you do not have to leave your family behind.

Man Is to Set the Moral Example for the Family

That means the man should set the example in the home. Now there is a dirty lie the Devil started and some people pass it along. Sometime ago I heard a preacher say, "There never was a man in the world good enough to marry a nice, clean, decent, Christian girl." What a silly statement! Lots of men are just as clean in their thoughts, in their lives, in their conscience, as devoted in their prayer life as any women. And they ought to be.

People say, "Well, a woman must walk straight. But a man is a man, and you expect him to curse a little, and drink a little, and commit some small sins. Of course you wouldn't want a woman to."

God has one standard, and you sorry, good-for-nothing, you alibing, excuse-making, dirty sinners who blame your sins on nature—listen, if you do not walk straight, you are not fit to marry a decent girl. Any man who does not say to his wife, "Come on, live just as good as I do and you will be fine"; any man who does not say to his own little girls, "Come on, you live as clean as I do. You pray as I do. You try to serve God. You talk as decently and as clean as I do and you will be all right";—If a man does not set that kind of standard, he is not a good Christian and not a good husband or father. God intended the man to set the pattern in the home.

"Well, Brother Rice, I sure hate to see a woman smoke." So do I. It is bad. Like my friend Sam Morris said, "How would you like every time you kissed your wife to smell a camel!" Well, that is pretty bad. There sure would be hell to pay in my house if I found my wife or one of my girls smoking.

I sat down in a little restaurant, a lunch counter, in Wheaton one time, and ordered a glass of milk and a sandwich. A lady (well, a woman at least) sat down on a stool beside me, opened her purse, took out a package of cigarettes, shook one out, tapped the end of it, and put it in her mouth, then lit it and blew the smoke in my face. I got up and moved, for I didn't want anybody to think that hussy belonged to me. I think it is pretty bad for a woman to smoke cigarettes. The fact is, it is nearly as bad as for a man, but not quite, for a man is the head of the wife, and the man is made in the image and glory of God. And God intends a man to set the pattern.

Which is worse—for us to have in the White House (like we did have with Harry Truman, a "good" Southern Baptist) a bourbon-drinking, cursing, Hell-raising, slandering, socialist President, or some poor guy down here on a creek, a colored man or poor white trash who drinks bootleg stuff? Which is morally the worse —the man in the White House, trusted and honored and before the world as an example; or this poor fellow down here? The fellow with the biggest opportunity and the greatest responsibilities is most accountable. Is that right? Yes, sir.

Which is worse—for the teacher, whom everyone respects, to go wrong, or some immature young pupil? It is worse for the teacher than for the pupil. Which is worse then—the father or the child? If the father goes wrong, that is worse. Which is worse—the husband or the wife? If the husband goes wrong morally, that is worse. He takes his family with him.

I was raised in the aristocratic South. My grandfather was captain in the Confederate Army, and I tell you, we thought the Rices were somebody. Dad used to remind us, "Boys, no Rice was ever arrested. None of our family ever spent a night in jail." When one of us would ride off out in that rough West Texas country, Dad would say, "Son, remember whose boy you are."

I grew up in the South where we respected women. No woman in our family hitched up her own horse to the buggy. They had fine horses to ride, but some man saddled them. None of the women folk of our family went into the field to chop cotton. The men worked like slaves, but not the women. We honored them.

They used to say, "The women will uphold the standards of the race." You thought so. They won't do it. The women are going like the men. And if the men curse, the women are going to curse. If the men drink, the women are going to drink. That is sad, but you had as well face it. It is a silly, foolish, devilish idea that a man can live in sin, yet his family stay fine. What we need to realize is that the women are going to follow the men, and the children are going to follow the women and the men.

God's plan is for man to lead the way in his home.

Men in the Home Are to Lead Spiritually

Spiritually then, the man ought

to lead in spiritual matters. That's God's plan. Some man says, "My wife has time to read the Bible, I don't. I've got to make a living."

Do you know what the Bible requires on this matter in I Corinthians 14:34,35? If any of you women should have a question, just keep quiet; don't disturb the service. Wait until you get home and ask your own husband that Bible question. Of course, it is good for a woman to have the help of pastors and others, but that Scripture requires that every man should be a good Bible student and should be able to inform and teach and help his own family in the Word of God, the Bible. A man is to be the spiritual leader of the home.

"Well, I don't like it," you say. Like it or lump it, you will meet God on that basis. That is God's plan.

How We Caught the Infidel Husband

Years ago I was in revival campaign at Duke, Oklahoma. The Baptist church and the Methodist church got together and we put up a big tabernacle. It was midwinter, and we made the tabernacle bigger than would hold the whole population of the town. They came from all over the county. People said, "When Harry Sadler shows used to come here, he didn't put up a tent this big. You can't fill this."

I said, "Watch and see." Since it was mid-winter, we put in four big furnaces to heat it. How the crowds came! And hundreds were saved.

One night a fellow came with his wife and sat down near the back. That night I waded in on worldly church members—you can't tell the difference, they stink like the Devil's crowd, go to the same lewd picture shows, take the same bloody, ungodly oaths—he liked that; I was picking on the crowd he liked to pick on himself.

So the next night he came back and sat halfway down toward the front. That night I was preaching to bring revival, a moral revolution, and house cleaning—still preaching to Christians. You will not have much revival if you do not have a house cleaning. If you do not reach the people of God, you won't reach the world.

He liked it so well the second night that the third night he came back and sat on the second seat. I was not plagued with a microphone then, and I didn't have too many inhibitions, so I jumped off the platform and on the front seat down there and was preaching away that night on the Christian home: "Any man who leaves it on the slender shoulders of his wife to carry the burdens of the home, to have thanks at the table, to have family altar, to get the children to Sunday School, to whip the children and make them mind, and turn them out in decent citizenship—any man who leaves all that on his wife is not fit to have a home. He is a slacker, a shirker a quitter."

I looked down at this fellow looking up to me and his mouth was wide open. He was dressed up; his hair was slicked down, his face was ruddy. I thought, "Here is a good Baptist deacon or

Methodist steward, so I will prove it by him." So I said, "Isn't that so, brother?"

He turned a little redder than usual. I said again, "Any man who leaves it on the slender shoulders of his wife to carry the burdens of the home and to have thanks at the table and family worship, and take the children to Sunday School, and to whip them and make them mind, and turn them out to be good Christians and good citizens—any man who leaves that to his wife is a slacker, a shirker, a quitter, and not fit to have a good home. Isn't that so?" I said, "Come on, isn't that so?"

He said, "I guess so."

I said. "You don't guess anything about it. You know that is so."

He said, "Yes, I know that is so."

I went on preaching. After the service the Methodist preacher came to me wringing his hands (I hope the Lord will forgive me for all the pastors I have scared out of ten years' growth!). "Oh, Brother Rice, why did you do it?"

"Why did I do what?"

"That old infidel—he came three times. That is the first time in twenty years he has ever heard any preacher more than once. So what do you do? You get him down in the second seat, stand right in front of him, put your finger under his nose and call him a slacker and a shirker and a quitter and tell him he is not fit to have a family. Oh, he will never come back!"

I said, "An infidel? I thought he was a Baptist deacon or a Methodist steward."

"Why, no. He runs down the churches and slanders God and deceives young people, and all that kind of business. He came and there might have been some chance, but he is gone and will never come back."

"Well," I said, maybe he won't come back, but he will know one thing: he heard one preacher, a prophet of God, and he got both barrels of the shot gun at one time. Besides that, I had him where the wool was short and made him admit in public that it was so. So if I never see him, then I have cleared my soul."

But the next night he came again with his little timid wife. He didn't escort her down the aisle with southern courtesy; I saw him come through the door and he got his wife by the wrist and they marched down to the second seat, as if to say, "Okay, so what? If anybody doesn't like it, speak up. I don't care. I am going to come and hear it anyhow." It was just an antagonistic attitude, but the point was, he had to hear the rest of it.

I preached some message to sinners that Saturday night. I poured out my soul, then gave the invitation. I got down on the front seat and said, "Who here will come tonight and say, 'I am a sinner, I here and now turn my back on sin, I put my trust in Jesus Christ, I take Him as my Saviour and claim him.' Will you come?" While they were singing I leaned over and whispered to this man: "Say, you didn't hold your hand that you were a Christian." I didn't say, "You infidel, I caught up with you." I said, "You didn't hold your hand that you were a Christian."

He said, "Me a Christian? Good night, no! I am not a Christian."

"Well," I said, "Look here, your hair is getting gray. You don't have much time to flirt with God. You are going to be in Heaven or Hell pretty soon. You had better make up your mind." I whispered to him and he whispered back as the crowd went on singing.

He said, "Preacher, listen. If I thought God would take a dirty old crook like me, I would come in a minute.

I said, "Here, let me show you what He said. 'Him that cometh to me I will in no wise cast out.'"

He said, "Well, if I thought He would take me . . . "

I said, "Shut up! Don't say *if* when God said He would do it. If God said He would take you, He will take you. Do you want Him?"

He said, "Yes."

"Then will you say, 'Jesus died for me. I am an old sinner. I will trust Him'?"

"Will you take my hand on it?"

He gripped my hand, a big old blacksmith type of fellow, and I said, "Do you trust Him?"

"Yes, sir."

"Do you mean it for good and forever?"

"Yes, sir."

"Okay. What about telling these people publicly?"

He said to me, "Brother Rice, listen. For twenty years my wife here beside me has been going to the First Christian Church by herself. Every Sunday morning she gets up and tries to get some of our big family of boys to go with her, but they usually won't do it. I get the Sunday paper and sit around in my stocking feet, and talk about the churches and the preachers and ask about this thing, this contradiction, and that and the other. I make fun and she stubbornly but bravely goes down to her own church. She has been going alone twenty years." He said, "Preacher, would it be all right if I didn't go up there now and claim it? If I can wait until tomorrow morning, I will get up and go with my wife where she has been going by herself, and claim the Lord publicly right down there with her. Would that be all right?"

I replied, "I never before told anybody they could wait ten minutes about claiming the Lord, but I believe that is okay. You go to it."

We went on with the invitation and several people were saved, but he didn't come forward. He didn't even tell his wife.

Next morning, Sunday morning, he got up early and said, "Hey, boys! Everybody roll out. We are all going to church today."

"Good night! What has happened to the old man?" My, all the washing of neck and ears and shining of shoes and, "Who's got my good shirt?" They got the boys ready and all went to church. The little woman was so happy and nearly in tears, not quite knowing all about it, but knowing it must be good. They went to church and the pastor preached the Gospel and gave an invitation, and this fellow went right out publicly and claimed the Lord. And since it was the First Christian Church, they baptized him before dinner! I don't care; if you have something really to be baptized about, the sooner the better. I don't like to bury one until he is dead, you understand. But after he is dead, we should bury him before he begins to stink! So they baptized him and he came home. That night he said to me in the big tabernacle, "You know, Brother Rice, I never was as much an infidel as I made out like."

Listen, you men! God help you to set out to lead your families. Joshua said, "As for me and my house, we will serve the Lord."

II. Wife's Place in the Home

Now what is the woman's place? I can't take much time for it, and I don't think I need so much time. If you men do right about this, you can teach your women. Oh, they will always have a little rebellion, like you have, because of the carnal nature, but what is a woman's place?

God Told Eve, "Thy Desire Shall Be to Thy Husband, and He Shall Rule Over Thee"

Go back yonder to the Garden of Eden when sin came in. Now you have to have law where there is sin. You have to have discipline and leadership and rulership. So God said to the woman, "I will greatly multiply thy sorrow and thy conception; in sorrow thou shalt bring forth children; and thy desire shall be to thy husband, and he shall rule over thee" (Gen. 3:16).

Some woman says, "I don't want anybody ruling over me." I have often felt that way, too. I would rather drive as fast as I think is wise instead of driving as fast as a sign says, or a policeman says. But we have to have policemen, laws, and speed limits.

Another says, "I don't want to mind anybody."

Yes, the prodigal son felt that way, too. That is why he left home. The Devil fell from Heaven as an archangel because he did not want to mind anybody. He said, "I am going to set my throne above the throne of God . . . . This business of bowing and scraping and doing everything I am told." Sinners go to Hell because they say, "We will not have this man to reign over us. I will not bow the knee to Jesus; will not call Him my Lord; will not give up the reins of my heart."

And I have had that trouble, too, sister. That is just the old devilish, carnal nature. But if you are a good wife or a good Christian, you have to have victory over that. No woman is a good Christian who is not a good wife. That is right. The woman's first human duty is to her husband. She is joined to him as one body. She is to obey him. The Scripture says, "Thy husband shall rule over thee."

Wives To Be Subject to Husband As Unto the Lord Jesus

"That is way back in the Old Testament," you argue.

Yes, but fortunately the God who wrote the Old Testament wrote a New Testament, too. So in Ephesians, chapter 5, beginning with verse 22, the Lord has a word here about wives and husbands and the home. 'Be subject to your own husband as unto the

Lord,' the Scripture says. The scriptural plan is that the wife is to be subject to the husband.

Obedient Wives Can Win Their Husbands

"But Brother Rice, my husband isn't even a Christian."

I know, but the Bible fits all cases. So I Peter, chapter 3, says, "Likewise, ye wives, be in subjection to your own husbands; that, if any obey not the word . . . ." Do you have a husband who won't listen to the Bible, who doesn't obey Christ? " . . . if any obey not the word, they also may without the word be won by the conversation of the wives." And the word translated *conversation* here in the old King James translation meant *daily living, manner of life*. So let them be won by the manner of life of the wives. These men who do not obey the Word may be won "while they behold your chaste conversation coupled with fear."

You see, the Scripture makes it clear that a woman who has an unsaved husband is to be obedient to that husband. Why not? Do you think a Christian woman ought to lie? You promised to love, honor and obey, didn't you? Do you think a Christian woman ought to break that holy marriage bond and vow? Some of you women have prayed for your husbands to be saved, but God won't answer your prayers. I will tell you why. You are a rebel against God and you live a lie every day. You lied to God, you lied to that bridegroom, you lied to the public when you were married. You didn't set out to obey that husband. God is not going to put an endorsement on your rebellion and sin.

"Well, but I am going to serve the Lord," someone declares.

But there is no way to serve the Lord without setting out to obey the authorities that God put over you. Do you think a man is a better Christian for being a lawbreaker? That a child is a better Christian if he scorns his dad and mother and lives in rebellion and self-will? Or that a wife is a better Christian because she ignores the plain command of the Bible?

But a woman says, "I have to go to church. A good Christian ought to go to Church." The Bible nowhere tells you how much to go to church, but it dead-sure says to obey your husband.

"If I were to obey my husband, he would have me out drinking and all that."

Do you think so? God said he may be won by the conversation of the wife. I would rather take God's Word than yours. Besides, yours is just an alibi because you don't really want to do what you promised God you would do. And if you had a sissy preacher perform the ceremony who took out what God put in about the marriage ceremony and if he didn't ask you to love, honor and *obey*, God still has it in. You are accountable to God and not the preacher. And you had better set out to live by it.

"Oh, it won't work," you say,

Tell God it won't work. I didn't write it, I am just preaching it. As far as I have found out, the Bible plan works.

"But don't you think one ought to put Christ first?"

Certainly you ought to put Christ first, but that won't make you a lawbreaker and a rebel. The truth is that duties never do conflict, and God is going to help you do right. Anytime by faith and love you set out to obey Jesus Christ, you will find it turns out well.

I wish I could tell you of many, many cases where good women have come to me with tears of joy. They tell how they quit their rebellion and how their husbands' love began to warm toward them and they began to be kind and make sure they were happy and then to go to church with them and then to come to Christ. God's way works. Wives, be subject to your husbands.

I hasten on.

III. Correction and Discipline of Children

What about children? There is much to be said and I don't dare to take much time, but children are to obey their parents in the Lord, for this is right (Eph. 6:1). When Joy was three years old she used to say, "Children, go 'bey your parents in the Lord." And then very triumphantly she would say, "For this is right! This is right!" And it is right!

"In the Discipline and Admonition of the Lord"

To fathers Ephesians 6 says: "But bring them up in the nurture and admonition of the Lord." That sounds like "feed them well and advise them." But in the Greek the word *nurture* means more than that. It is *discipline* in the old sense. The same Greek word that Pilate used when he said about Jesus, "I will chastise him and let him go," is the word used here in the Greek about children being brought up in the nurture or discipline of the Lord.

You may say, "I don't believe in whipping them. I just believe in withdrawing some privileges." But God plainly specifies the *rod* of correction, and there is no better way than God's way.

"Brother Rice, I am afraid you will break the will of the little one," some parent declares.

As a man of long experience with little children, I will tell you something for your own good. The danger is not that you will break the will of that little helpless one whom God in mercy put in your care, but that he will break your will.

You say, "Oh, the little innocent...."

No, no! Not innocent. Dear, sweet, precious, immortal blessings wrapped up in little body, mind and soul—oh, infinitely lovely, but not innocent. They have the devil in them and if you don't whip part of it out, it will stay in them.

If You Love Him, Chasten Him!

Listen to what the Word says in Proverbs, chapter 13, verse 24: "He that spareth his rod hateth his son: but he that loveth him chasteneth him betimes."

"I love my boy too much," you say. "Brother Rice, you must not love your children if you whip them and make them do what you say, see that they get up when called the first time, and say, 'Yes, sir.' "

I loved my six girls enough so I didn't want one of them to be a harlot. I didn't want any of them to marry a drunkard, nor go to the dogs.

"Well, you can't tell how children will turn out," you say.

I can. I didn't leave mine for somebody else to turn out. By God's grace I helped turn mine out.

I have heard people say, "When they are little they step on your toes, and when they get older they step on your heart."

Not mine. I didn't put up with them stepping on my toes when they were little, and they are not going to step on my heart when I am old because I looked after that by the blessing of God and with what help I could get and prayer and tears and love and teaching the Word and discipline. We worked at it. But "he that loveth his son chasteneth him betimes." Now if you think you are so smart, you had better get a little Divine wisdom. Here is real love that turns out happily.

And here is a mother who says, "I love my child."

No you don't. You love yourself and your own ease. You don't have the integrity and the character and the conviction to do right about it. Then you pretend that mush is love. That is not love. If that is love, then an old sow loves her pigs as much as you love your child. That is not right. Christian love is more that that.

"Chasten Thy Son While There Is Hope"

Again the Scripture says in Proverbs 19:18, "Chasten thy son while there is hope, and let not thy soul spare for his crying." Chasten thy son while there is hope. When? While he is young. Begin in time. How soon should you whip a little child? I don't know.

I wonder, Dr. Lee (Dr. R. G. Lee was in the audience), did you know B. B. Crimm? You surely did. He was a Texas cowboy evangelist. I don't say this is authoritative; I am giving one good man's opinion, but B. B. Crimm said, "Personally I don't think you ought to whip girl babies as early as boy babies. I don't think you ought to whip a girl until she is three weeks old! A boy you can begin on as soon as he is born!"

I tell you this: if by the time a child is a year old and you can't say "No," and he stops; if you can't say, "Don't touch that," and make it stick; if you can't put him to bed and say, "Now go to sleep," and he goes to sleep, then you have coming later on some heartache and tears and gray hairs.

The Scripture says about this matter, "Chasten thy son while there is hope." Anybody who begins in time, with love and consistency and prayer, and stays with it, can turn out good, honest boys and girls, get them saved early, make them decent, clean citizens. But you have to begin in time. "Chasten thy son while there is hope, and let not thy soul spare for this crying."

"Well, Brother Rice, I don't know what is the matter with mine," you lament.

I know what is the matter. You don't even lay a hand on him until you get so mad you grit your teeth, then spat him a little. Then he yells bloody murder and you have to buy three ice cream cones and take him to see Grandma to get him to stop crying! Listen! If you went at it like my dad did, you might get better results. My dad, when he whipped, whipped until you cried, then whipped until you stopped.

You say, "Sometimes you can't."

If my dad was ahold of you, you would find a way to stop. If you will listen to me this morning, we will change the face of your part of America. I am for revivals, but not for this little nice business of revivals that make everybody feel good; pat them on the back, and have a few testimonies and handshakes, and so on, then you go and live like the Devil at home. If it doesn't revolutionize your life, then you haven't gotten enough.

Stripes Cleanse the Character

Proverbs 20:30 says, "The blueness of a wound cleanseth away evil: so do stripes the inward parts of the belly."

"You don't take that literally?" you say.

Yes.

"Actual stripes?"

Yes.

"Would you whip a little child until you left marks on him?"

Maybe. I have had many a mark left on me. Yes, Sir. I remember when Grace was three years old. (When she was extra stubborn her mother used to say, "Just like her daddy." Now how in the world did she get that idea?) Once a matter came up, and I do not now remember what it was I told her to do, but she was stubborn. She said, "No." She wouldn't. She was only three years old, and I insisted but she didn't do it. Finally I waded in on the place the Lord prepared on little girls for this business. I spanked with my open hand until we got the thing settled. The next day I saw on that tender little skin the blue marks of the print of my fingers, and I went aside and wept. I nearly had to whip my wife, too, by the way. I said, "Lord, I didn't say I knew how. I haven't made any claims. You gave me the child. All I know is this—You help me and I am going to do it." Thanks be to God, it works. The blueness of a wound cleanseth away evil.

Now I believe in love and prayers. A woman came to Dr. Bob Jones, Sr. and said, "Dr. Bob, will you pray for my fourteen-year-old boy who is already drinking and cussing? He is out late at night, and he scoffs at me and won't listen. He is breaking my heart. Dr. Bob, will you pray for my boy?"

Wise Dr. Bob asked, "How old did you say he is?"

"Fourteen. Dr. Bob, he drinks and cusses and won't mind, and he is breaking my heart. Will you pray for him?"

"No, I will not."

"Why, Dr. Bob! You won't pray for him?"

He answered, "Why should I waste my time praying for a

thing you could fix in ten or fifteen minutes with a stick, if you really meant business?"

Now I am for praying, but praying without obeying is hypocrisy. It is all right to pray, provided you live like you talk. And if you don't act in accordance with your prayers, God is not going to bless you.

"When He is Old, He Will Not Depart From it"

Here is Proverbs 22:6, "Train up a child in the way he should go: and when he is old, he will not depart from it." ". . . *even* when he is old," the American Standard Version says. The Bible does not mean that if he lives like the Devil he will later come back to God's way. That is what people say, but that is not what God said. God said he won't leave it. You can raise up a child and train him for God, get him saved and living right.

I preached in the Tabernacle Baptist Church near Gainesville, Texas, when I was in Southwestern Seminary as a student pastor. When I preached on "The Home" one man said, "You have got to go home with me."

I said, "I have a date with Mr. White."

But he pleaded, "Excuse yourself, please. You must go with me."

And I said to Mr. White, "This brother is in trouble. He wants me to go; will you excuse me?"

"Yes."

I went home with him. We stopped out in the yard and his wife got out of the car and went into the house. He said, "Brother Rice, what you preached this morning is not so."

I said, "Watch your step, old boy. Nobody in my church tells me what I preach is not so. What I preached this morning is the Word of God."

"Brother Rice, it isn't so. You said if you train up a child in the way he should go, when he is old, he will not depart from it."

I said, "You've got hold of the wrong fellow. I didn't say that. God said it."

"Well then, the Bible isn't so."

I said, "Now we are going to have this settled, because I will not be a pastor of a man and in a church where people say the Bible isn't true. What is wrong?"

"I don't want to tell you."

"You will tell me, or I will go get your wife right now and we will have it out. Yes, you are going to tell me."

"Well, my boy is in the state penitentiary in Huntsville, Texas, but I am not to blame. I know I did raise him right."

"All right. Since you have made God a liar and challenged your pastor on this thing, let's see if you raised him right. For one thing, did you have family worship in your home?"

"Look here, Brother Rice, I am on the farm. I have got to work hard. You city people may have time to fool around with things like that, but I have to get up early and make a living. We didn't have time to waste." And so he didn't have any family worship, and his boy was in the state penitentiary now.

I said to him, "Here is another thing. Did you whip that boy and make him mind? Did you make him get up the first time you called and make him say, 'Yes, Sir' and 'Yes, Ma'am.' Did you make him jump when you spoke to him?"

He said, "Now look here, Brother Rice. Not all children are alike. My boy was nervous and high-strung and you just couldn't bear down on him like you could on some people."

(Incidentally, I was nervous and high-strung too. I tell you the truth, sometimes I would get so mad I would see red and I would get so dizzy I would have to sit down somewhere. But fortunately on this matter I had a dad who got nervouser than I. We soon got that fixed, you know.)

"Now listen," I said. "One more thing. You have charged God and the Bible as not being true. You have a boy who went to the dogs and is in the state penitentiary for a major crime. You never had family worship, never whipped him to make him mind. Let me ask you, did you ever try to win that boy to Christ? Did you ever say, 'Son, we are going to have a revival up here at the Tabernacle Church and I want you to come and get saved. We trusted in Jesus, your mother and I; now I want you to put your trust in Jesus and get saved'? Did you ever try to get that boy saved?"

He said, "Now look here, Brother Rice, I am a Baptist. I am no Methodist. I don't believe in dragging little children in when they don't know what it is about."

So now his boy was in the penitentiary. If any of you Methodists here want to take that kind of Baptist, you can have him as far as I am concerned. But do you believe that boy was raised in the way he should go? No. By God's grace you don't have to give up your children.

Moses was down in Egypt and Pharaoh said, "You go, but leave the women and children. You can go, but leave all the flocks and herds. You don't want to get out with them."

Moses said, "Not a hoof will be left behind." And I have said to God, "Lord, of these six girls You gave me, by God's grace the Devil is not going to have a one." Not a hoof will be left behind. You don't have to let the Devil get your children like Lot did.

IV. Making Christ the Head of the Home

How can I make Christ the head of the home?

Always Have Thanks at Meals

First of all, have thanks at the table. We ought to take time to thank God. You don't know how much that means. It somehow makes a concept of life that is proper. When I was pastor at First Baptist Church in Shamrock, Texas, Grace, my oldest daughter, was just a little thing about four or five years old. Mother said, "Lunch is ready. Come to the table." I came to the table, but Grace had to go wash her face. She had the idea of washing your face without getting it wet, which is pretty difficult! She would dip the tips of three fingers in the water and shake the water off and get a little spot on her cheek and go around and around. It takes a good while to wash your face that way!

Finally Mrs. Rice said, "Let's go ahead and return thanks. She'll get here when she can."

So we had thanks. After a while Grace got to the table. So I said, "Honey, do you want some potatoes, nice potatoes?"

"Daddy, we didn't pray."

"Yes we did, honey, before you got here. Would you like some potatoes?"

"Daddy, we didn't pray."

"Yes, we did, honey, before you got here. Would you like some potatoes?"

"Daddy . . . " And her lips began to quiver. "Daddy, we didn't pray."

I said to Mrs. Rice, "She ought not to eat without praying, and we will never leave the children out from this time on."

You had better thank God every time you eat. You had better teach your children to thank God for everything good they get.

Family Worship With Bible and Circle of Prayer

That is not all. You ought to have family worship. What do you mean? I mean you ought to have regularly some time every day when the whole family (those old enough to read) reads the Bible together and prays together. At least those who are Christians ought to do that.

When our children were little we started to have family worship at night. I would preach and get in about 10:30 or 11:00 at night. We would wake the children, prop them up in bed and try to get their eyes open and read to them a chapter and pray. We prayed, "Now, Lord, help us live right today," but the day was already gone, you know. So that was not the best time to do it. Then we agreed to have it before breakfast. But the soft-boiled eggs got to be hard-boiled, and the toast burned and had to be scraped, and the hot chocolate got cold. That wouldn't work.

So we decided on right after breakfast. Now for many, many years what a blessed and happy institution it has been in our home. We get done with breakfast and I say, "Girls, get your Bibles." Everyone gets her Bible. (Now, 1960, all are married.) From the time they were in the third grade so they could practice and spell out one verse, the girls have read, too. And a wonderful thing happened—they early got to be the best readers in their class and got a passion for reading and literature, etc. That was a by-product of it.

I would read two verses, then the next one two verses and the next one two verses. So we always started on an odd number, and everybody read. You may not know it, but girls can look as innocent and pious and be thinking, "What ribbon will I wear today?" or "I wonder if I will see that boy at school today." So they have got to watch in order to see where they are going to read next. And everybody around the table read two verses. If it was a short chapter, we read two of them, and if it was long, we read the chapter, two verses each, around and around and around.

Sometimes I would ask, "Mary

Lloys, what verse in this chapter do you like best?" Or, "Let's all memorize verse 7." Sometimes we would sing a chorus and then pray. I would pray and the next girl, and around. The girls prayed from the time they were little girls, and nearly every one of them started out like this: "Lord, we thank You for this 'brefus' food." They all prayed, and then I prayed again. I got to pray three times every morning at my house —when I returned thanks at the table, then when I started the prayer and then when I closed the prayer. It sure was good. I hate for my family to all be gone. How I miss that little bit of Heaven, that little church of our family worship! Take time.

Teach Your Children the Bible

What else? Teach your children the Bible. At our house we memorized a lot of Scripture, though not as much as we should have. Every Easter Sunday morning we said from memory the 28th chapter of Matthew. Christmas we would say over part of the second chapter of Luke.

We learned the 1st Psalm, the 15th Psalm, 23rd Psalm, 24th Psalm 34th Psalm (I memorized the 37th Psalm. I don't know whether the family did or not), the 100th Psalm, 103rd, 121st, 126th, and the 127th, as I remember. Then we memorized the Beatitudes; John the third chapter; I Corinthians, chapter 13; Philippians, chapter 4; Romans, chapter 8; Romans, chapter 12, and some others I don't think of at this minute; hundreds and hundreds of verses.

Oh, teach your children the Word of God. You can.

You say, "They can't learn it." Listen, that child who is not over seven years old or ten years old will spend more time than you will give to teach them to memorize. My little granddaughter, Faith, memorized many, many verses to earn a trip to camp. Yes, they will take it. You had better do it. Teach your children the Word of God.

And then make Christ first. You cannot do that unless you let Christ in to be the Boss and Lord over the whole business.

"Christ Is the Head of This House"

Years ago I was in south Texas at revival services and I tried to win a man to Christ who was of the Campbellite persuasion. He did not like Baptists and he did not like me. He did not want to be saved. I prayed about it. One day I heard he had a new baby at his house, so I said to my wife, "The Lord has played it into my hands. I am going down there. I will get that fellow saved, by God's grace. You watch and see."

I went and knocked and he came to the door. "Say, I heard the good news. I hear you have a baby."

"Yes."

"I heard another thing, that he is a boy. I have a house full of girls, but not a single son. They tell me you have a boy."

"Yes, Sir. And he weighs eight pounds. He's a whopper. And he's a good one, Brother Rice."

"That's fine. Could I see him?"

"Yes, Sir. Come in, come in." He took me back to the bedroom and said to his wife, "Brother Rice wants to see our boy. He's got only girls. We've got a boy and Brother Rice wants to see our boy."

She reached over to the side and got the bundle in a little blue blanket with rabbits on it and began to unfold it. She opened it until you could see a little bit of a red-faced, bald-headed, little fellow I said, "My, isn't he nice!"

The wife answered. "Well, others may not think he is so pretty, but I think he is awful pretty."

I said, "Well, he is an immortal soul. And he will be a man. A man is somebody, and that is wonderful. Say, what about me having a prayer for him? Would you like me to pray for God to bless him?"

"Yes, I would. Yes, Sir."

I said to the father, "Is that all right?"

"Yes, Sir. That's right. Pray for him."

This was kind of a hit below the belt. I said, "All right now; what shall we do? Shall we pray for him to grow up and be a Christian, get converted and live for God and go to Heaven, or shall we pray for him to drink and curse and follow the steps of his father? Which shall we do?"

The wife was shocked, and she said, "My, I never thought of that. I want him to be a good man, to live right and go to Heaven. Pray for him to be a Christian."

"All right. We will pray for him to be converted and be a Christian. But who is going to win him to Christ and teach him how to be a Christian? Who is going to do that?"

That woman, with tears in her eyes, said, "I never thought of that. Who will? I am not a Christian; his dad is not a Christian. You had better pray for me. I don't know how to raise a boy to be a Christian. You had better pray for me to get converted and be a Christian."

I said, "All right. We will ask the Lord Jesus to come into your heart and save you so you will be a Christian and can lead the boy."

I turned to the man who was sitting in a cane-bottom chair and asked, "Are you a Christian?" (I knew. I had talked to him five days before and he wouldn't be saved, so I knew.) But I asked, "Are you a Christian?"

"No, Brother Rice, I am not." He was subdued by this time.

I said, "What is that motto doing over there?" (On a wall motto it said, "Christ is the Head of this House, the Unseen Guest at Every Meal, the Silent Listener at Every Conversation.") "What about that motto?"

"Well . . . "

"Christ is not the Head of this house and you know it."

"Brother Rice, now listen. I didn't mean to blaspheme; I wasn't poking fun. I saw that in a store and thought it was pretty and thought my wife would like it, so I bought it and put it up, but I will take it down. I don't have any business with that up there. I am not fit to have that in my home. I will take it down."

I said, "Wait. Why not ask Jesus to come in and be the Head of the whole house? Ask Him to save the little boy through you and his mother's influence. Let's ask Him to come into your heart."

He said, "I wish you would." He put his face down in his hands and tears dripped between his fingers. Then that little mother held the baby up so close, and her lips just trembled and tears ran down her face, and I prayed and she cried, and the angels stopped playing their harps to listen. And God listened, and Jesus Christ came into that woman's heart and the man's heart. He came into that house to be the Head of the house.

There is no way to make Christ the Head of the house unless you take Him in your heart and trust Him as your Saviour.

Listen, I am taking a little extra time because I want this settled. How many of you men here will say, "If Joshua ought to say that, I ought to say it. As for me and my house, we will serve the Lord"? Is that right, men? How many of you men have already said, "By God's grace I am setting out to lead my family for God"? All right, stand up just a minute. Wait a minute. Are you willing to restate that vow? Are you? Are you willing to say again, "As for me and my house, I will live for God, I will lead my wife, my children; I will set my standards for the family, by God's grace"? That will take grace. It will take help. We are awfully poor sticks to be leading families, but we are all God has for leading the family. How many of the rest of you men say, "Well, I ought to. I will try"? Will you?

One man came to me once and said, "Brother Rice, I couldn't stand up. I have a four-year-old boy, and I smoke. I don't want that boy to do that. You are going to have to pray for God to clean me up and help me. But I have got to do it, because I can't have my boy doing like I have been doing." And I did pray for him.

Now how many will say, "I am weak, I may make mistakes, but God being my helper, I say like Joshua, I will serve the Lord. I will try to lead my family for God. I am weak but I will undertake what I ought to undertake, God helping me"? Don't say it unless you mean worship in the home, discipline in the home, godly living in the home. Come on, men. Who will join us? Come on, stand up with us. I will ask your wife to stand by you in a minute. That is right. Come on, men. Come on, will you? If *I* ought to do that, *you* ought to do it. Is that right? If I ought to do it, you ought to do it. Come on, will you? (Most of the men stood.)

All right, how many women here will say, "Yes, I want that kind of home. I am going to stand by my husband in that kind of home. I will try to be subject to him and I will try to be a good Christian and try to help raise the children right. I will try to make it a Christian home"? Come on, stand up by your husband. Come on, stand up where you are. You good wives—God bless you. (Most women stand.) I knew you would do it.

Here are some children. Yesterday afternoon a twelve-year-old girl was saved. Last night a thirteen-year-old boy was saved. And then there was a little girl saved over here and then a man here. Forty-five or fifty came to get assurance of salvation. Here is a widow who doesn't have family. All right, will you say, "Whatever home I live in, I will try to help make it a Christian home"? Here is a young boy or girl who says, "I am not married. I don't have my own home but I will try to stand by those who have a home." Come on, stand up with us. Will you say, "Whatever home I live in (if you don't have your own), at least I will try to make it Christian"? Some of you will have your own some day. Make it a Christian home.

Is there anybody here who will say, "Brother Rice, I don't know how to go all the way, but I do want Jesus to come in and take over"? You say, "Brother Rice, pray for me, and God helping me I will try to surrender to Jesus today the best I can." Come on. Can you say yes by standing up? We are going to have prayer now. Will you do that? Will you say yes by standing up? You say, "I haven't got it settled; I can't go all the way." Thank you brother; God bless you. "But I want Jesus to have His full sway. I ask you to pray God will give me grace." You hesitate about making a vow and pledge, but you do want God's best and you do, the best you know how, surrender and trust and give up to Jesus. Will you do that? Anybody else?

"Dear Lord, hear our vows. Come in power upon us, O God, today."

Serve God
Without Regard for Consequences

(SERMON PREACHED SUNDAY MORNING, DECEMBER 24, 1939, AT GALILEAN BAPTIST CHURCH, DALLAS. STENOGRAPHICALLY REPORTED.)

"Therefore I say unto you, Take no thought for your life, what ye shall eat, or what ye shall drink; nor yet for your body, what ye shall put on. Is not the life more than meat, and the body than raiment? Behold the fowls of the air: for they sow not, neither do they reap, nor gather into barns; yet your heavenly Father feedeth them. Are ye not much better than they? Which of you by taking thought can add one cubit unto his stature? And why take ye thought for raiment? Consider the lilies of the field, how they grow; they toil not, neither do they spin: And yet I say unto you, That even Solomon in all his glory was not arrayed like one of these. Wherefore, if God so clothe the grass of the field, which today is, and tomorrow is cast into the oven, shall he not much more clothe you, O ye of little faith? Therefore take no thought, saying, What shall we eat? or, What shall we drink? or, Wherewithall shall we be clothed? (For after all these things do the Gentiles seek:) for your heavenly Father knoweth that ye have need of all these things. But seek ye first the kingdom of God, and his righteousness; and all these things shall be added unto you. Take therefore no thought for the morrow: for the morrow shall take thought for the things of itself. Sufficient unto the day is the evil thereof."—Matt. 6:25-34.

Look at verse 25: "Therefore I say unto you, Take no thought for your life." Isn't that strange? "Take no thought...." Then the verse goes on to say, "nor yet for your life or your body." So take no thought for your life or your body. Read again verse 31: "Therefore take no thought, saying, What shall we eat? or, What shall we drink, or, Wherewithall shall we be clothed?"

Now verse 34: "Take therefore no thought for the morrow:

for the morrow shall take thought for the things of itself."

God says to "take no thought." Isn't that a strange thing—"take no thought"? As I meditated today and yesterday on the account of the Christmas story and the birth of Christ I was amazed at some things I found about the attitude of heart of those whom God saw fit to bless. So in connection with this Scripture, I will speak on this general theme of *Serving God Without Any Regard for Consequences*. We need to serve God on this basis, that our minds are already made up, that we already know that it pays to serve God and to put Him first We need to come to the point where we can say, "I will not worry about bread and meat, about friends, about whether I live or die. I am going to serve God *without any regard to the consequences*."

We Should Count the Cost and Settle It Once for All

Yes, there is such a thing as counting the cost, and the Saviour said plainly that we are to do that. The Bible commands us to sit down and count the cost whether we will be Christians. That is like a man who builds a tower. He must sit down first and see how much it will cost. It is like a man who starts war. He had better figure out whether with his ten thousand men he can meet the other king with twenty thousand, and if so, go ahead. If not, then send an ambassage desiring peace. Jesus said to count the cost about being a Christian.

Do you mean business? **Are you able to go right ahead and live for** God, with your mind made up to turn your back on sin and live for God? Christians ought to do that, but that is something that ought to happen just once. We should get it settled once for all, "I am for God; I can risk Him, and I will do what He says." After that, a Christian ought to come to the place where he can say, "I will not take thought for my life. I will not take thought for my body. I will not take thought for what I eat or drink or what I wear. I will not take thought for tomorrow, but will leave that with God. Already I have counted the cost and tried God, and already I have found it pays to serve Him. Already I have found God can be trusted. I can serve Him in the dark without knowing the future. I can serve God without a guarantee. I can serve God without any visible evidence as to how He will bring me out. I can serve God without any regard for the consequences."

We can count the cost, then having counted the cost, have our minds made up.

You men, how would you like to marry a woman who would say, "Yes," then before you can ever get married, you would have to reconvince her forty times? Then when finally you got married, she would say, "But I want to stay here and live with mother." And you would have to settle that question again. Then when the question came up of what kind of a house you would live in, she would say, "Well, if I can't have such and such a house, I think

I would be better off to go back home and live with mother." And every time you turn around the question comes up again. And all the time your wife stayed with you as your wife, it would have to be on the basis that you would fight it out again every day that you could give her more than her mother and dad could.

Or how would you like to live with a woman when it was an open question every day whether she could be true to you and live with you and wear your name?

Then what does God think about it when a man claims to be a Christian and every day the open question has to be argued out again about everything God ever tells him to do? How do you think God feels when He comes to a Christian and that Christian says, "Yes, Lord, I will follow You where You lead me, will go where You want me to go," then every time, even if it is only the proposition of ten cents out of one dollar, it has to be argued out and weighed all over again whether it pays to tithe, and you wonder if you can afford to do this and wonder how you can live if you do as God says?

Every time there is a chance to serve God, you have to put it under a microscope and check it very carefully to see whether it pays or not. And when you come to teach a Sunday School class, you have to weigh whether to give up shows and whether you can afford to be here every Sunday when you want to go see Mother. If you were God, would you like to have a bunch of Christians who were never settled whether they mean business or not, and every time God tells them to do something, it has to be fought out again?

What I am talking about this morning is that there ought to come a time when every Christian could settle once and for all, "I will serve God without regard to consequences. I h a v e already counted the cost and decided it is worth while." You ought to make up your mind that whatever comes tomorrow, you will be right in the will of God. God says to take no thought for tomorrow. Take no thought for your body. Take no thought of what you eat and drink. Take no thought! Wouldn't you like to serve God without regard to the consequences?

Mary Served God Without Taking Thought for Consequences

First, let me call your attention to those connected with the birth of Christ. Oh, how sweet is the story!

There was a virgin girl. One day as she sat alone I think she prayed. The angel of the Lord appeared to her and said, "Fear not, Mary." Read it in Luke 1:26-37.

Imagine how startled she was! Her face must have turned white as the angel appeared. And he said, "Fear not, Mary, thou hast found favour with God." She must have prayed a lot.

"And behold, thou shalt conceive in thy womb, and bring forth a son, and shalt call his name JESUS. He shall be great, and shall be called the Son of the Highest; and the Lord God shall give unto

him the throne of his father David: And he shall reign over the house of Jacob for ever: and of his kingdom there shall be no end."

But Mary said, "How can that be? How can I have a child? I am not married, and I am a pure, clean girl. I have never known a man after the flesh. How could I have a child?"

And the angel said, "The Holy Ghost shall come upon thee, and the power of the Highest shall overshadow thee: therefore also that holy thing which shall be born of thee shall be called the Son of God."

Do you suppose Mary stopped and figured, "If I become a mother when I am not married, there will come public shame on me. It is bound to be, and nobody will understand it. People won't believe what I tell them. And can I stand it or not?"

Did Mary go through all that argument? Did she weigh the whole thing? No, no. Mary said with a glad heart in that moment to the angel, "Be it unto me according to thy word." She said, "Oh, let it be just like you have said."

God sent Elisabeth to talk to Mary by the Holy Spirit. Elisabeth said, "Blessed art thou among women . . . because you believed what God said."

Mary didn't have to fight it all out and weigh the thing, count the cost. She didn't say, "Well, now wait! Let me see how it will turn out."

Mary gave herself to open and public shame for God's cause that she might bear in her body the body of the Baby Jesus and become the mother of the Son of God without regard to the consequences, taking no thought how it would turn out. She said, "Yes," and God brought it even as He said.

Joseph Disregarded the Shame and Misunderstanding to Take Mary and Rear Jesus

Take the case of Joseph. Joseph was troubled. Oh, how he loved Mary! Wouldn't you be, if your girl was such a pure, good girl, so bright? She was of noble lineage. She was of the house and lineage of David. She was a princess though poor and poverty stricken. She was such a pure and lovely woman that God selected this girl out of all the women in the world to be the mother of His Son. Don't you think you would have loved her? Oh, how Joseph loved her! When he was with her, she was timid and blushes covered her face, but she couldn't speak of it to him. But the outward evidence grew until finally Joseph could see that she was going to become a mother.

"Has Mary gone wrong?" He wept about the matter alone, but dared not mention it to her. He felt, "What can I do? If I reported her to the public authorities as an adulteress, she could be taken out and stoned. I wouldn't want to do that."

But in his sleep one night, in his troubled slumber, the angel of the Lord came to him and said:

"Joseph, thou son of David, fear not to take unto thee Mary thy wife: for that which is conceived

in her is of the Holy Ghost. And she shall bring forth a son, and thou shalt call his name JESUS: for he shall save his people from their sins. Now all this was done that it might be fulfilled which was spoken of the Lord by the prophet, saying, Behold, a virgin shall be with child, and shall bring forth a son, and they shall call his name Emmanuel, which being interpreted is, God with us."—Matt. 2:20-23.

And when Joseph was raised from sleep he took unto him Mary as his wife, and knew her not until she had brought forth her firstborn Son.

People don't say much about Joseph. He must have died before the Saviour was grown to manhood, for we never hear of him after Jesus was twelve years of age; but Joseph was a great man of God. That day when he woke out of his slumber and sat up on the edge of his couch, he said, "It is of God. I will not be afraid of the future. I will take Mary to my home as my wife and yet not my wife. I will take care of her. The Baby is not my baby, but I will take her home with me. Never mind what men say. The restraint and patience that is necessary—I will not mind it." So Joseph had no regard for the consequences. *He took no thought.* He did what God said.

The Wise Men Did Not Hesitate to Seem Foolish and Spend Money and Time for God

The wise men came from the East to see the Baby Jesus. They read in the book of Daniel the story of the coming Messiah. It was the only part of the Old Testament that they had over in Babylon, and was written by Daniel the prophet while there in the captivity. And the wise men read the ninth chapter of Daniel and knew that after the decree of Cyrus to rebuild Jerusalem, there would be sixty-nine weeks of years until the Messiah would come. And those sixty-nine weeks of years, four hundred and eighty-three years, had already come to pass, and now was the time for the promised King of the Jews. They were watching and ready, and when the star appeared they said, "It is His star, the evidence we have waited for."

The Holy Spirit told them the Saviour, the King of the Jews, was born. I do not know what tellings of good-by they had, who they put in charge of their business. I do not know what excuses they made to their wives and families about being gone so long and so far. They made arrangements and then perhaps mounted their camels and away they rode yonder toward the west from Babylon which was east, five hundred or six hundred miles, and they rode on around the northern part of the desert and across the Jordan River, and came to Jerusalem, and said, "Where is he that is born King of the Jews? for we have seen his star in the east, and are come to worship him."

They looked it up in the Bible, and the scribes said, "It must be Bethlehem, for Micah 5:2 says he will be born in Bethlehem." And, lo, the star appeared, and they came straight to the Baby Jesus and opened their treasures, gold and frankincense and myrrh. They left their gifts and went back home.

Can you imagine the expense of a journey that far when they had no cars, no trains, had no paved roads? It was from one nation to another nation, a nation of a strange language. Can you imagine the time it took—months, perhaps? Can you imagine the expense of it? They brought treasures along, gold, frankincense and myrrh. They came without any regard to the consequences. They took no thought for the morrow and served God with no reservations.

Shepherds Too Disregarded the Consequences to See the Baby Jesus

Remember the shepherds:

"And there were in the same country shepherds abiding in the field, keeping watch over their flock by night. And, lo, the angel of the Lord came upon them, and the glory of the Lord shone round about them: and they were sore afraid. And the angel said unto them, Fear not: for, behold, I bring you good tidings of great joy, which shall be to all people. For unto you is born this day in the city of David, a Saviour which is Christ the Lord. And this shall be a sign unto you; ye shall find the babe wrapped in swaddling clothes, lying in a manger. And suddenly there was with the angel a multitude of the heavenly host praising God and saying, Glory to God in the highest and on earth peace, good will toward men."—Luke 2:8-14.

Do you know what these men said? "Let us now go even unto Bethlehem, and see this thing which is come to pass which the Lord hath made known unto us."

What happened here shows that they didn't leave anybody to watch the sheep. They might have said, "Suppose a wolf gets the sheep," but nobody said anything like that. They never thought anything about that. If God had sent a Saviour, that is much more important than sheep. So they hotfooted it down to Bethlehem and found the Saviour. They walked in the stable there and found the Baby Jesus in the manger wrapped in swaddling clothes by the side of His mother. They forgot the consequences!

Then what did they do when they had seen the Saviour? Their hearts rejoiced, and they said, "It is true! It is true!" They didn't go back to the sheep. The Scripture said they went out praising God and glorifying God and told the good news. Then after they had told everybody they knew, they came back to find their sheep.

Were the sheep there when they got back, or not? The Bible does not say, because it didn't especially matter. For if a Saviour is born, what if a wolf did get a sheep! I imagine they were all there, all right, but if they were not, they didn't worry about it. They served God without regard for the consequences. They did what they ought to do for God without saying, "I wonder if the sheep will all be here?" No, no! They served God without any regard to the consequence. They took no thought. They believed it and God blessed them in it.

I wonder if we can't today make up our minds to start serving God without always taking thought, without always counting the cost!

The Three Hebrew Children Stayed True Without Regard to Consequences

Many other men in the Bible served God without counting the cost. Turn back to the book of Daniel. How rich it is. We need some iron in our blood like these men of God had.

Nebuchadnezzar built a great image, ninety feet high and nine feet wide, and the people must fall down and worship it. So he had all the orchestra, all the stringed instruments of every kind; the sackbut, the psaltery, the harps, etc., and when the orchestra played and the drums rolled, everybody was to bow down before the image which was set up in the plain of Dura, in the province of Babylon. But there were three men who didn't bow. Daniel was running the empire while the king was having a good time. But the three Hebrew children, Shadrach, Meshach, and Abednego, did not bow. While everybody was bowing down to the image, somebody peeked like some of you do when we pray. Somebody looked and saw the three Hebrew children, Shadrach, Meshach, and Abednego, standing straight up. They didn't bow down at all! A tattle-tale hotfooted it to the king and told him that the three men would not bow to the image. The king said, "Is it true?" He said, "Whoso falleth not down and worshippeth, that he should be cast into the midst of a burning fiery furnace."

Some Jews hadn't bowed down yet, and when Nebuchadnezzar was told this, "Nebuchadnezzar spake and said unto them, Is it true, O Shadrach, Meshach, and Abednego, do not ye serve my gods, nor worship the golden image which I have set up?" He told them that he was going to give them one more chance and if they worshipped not, he would cast them into the midst of a burning fiery furnace, seven times hotter than before, and they would not live a second. Listen to what they said:

"Shadrach, Meshach, and Abednego answered and said to the king, O Nebuchadnezzar, we are not careful to answer thee in this matter."

They didn't ask for time to consider the matter. "We are not careful to answer thee in this matter.

"If it be so, our God, whom we serve is able to deliver us from the burning fiery furnace, and he will deliver us out of thine hand, O king. But if not, be it known unto thee, O king, that we will not serve thy gods, nor worship the golden image which thou hast set up."

They said, "God is able to do it. He can and will, and if He does not, we won't do it anyway. We are not going to do it." They said, "Be it known unto thee, O king, that we will not serve thy gods, nor worship the golden image which thou hast set up."

Those folk were already voted. It is wonderful to find Christians who have already made up their minds. It is wonderful to find men who already know what they are going to do for God. If there comes a time of testing, they have already foreseen it, and say, "I don't care, God is able to deliver me. God can deliver me, and God will deliver me, but if He doesn't, I will do what He said anyway." So they said, "We are not going to bow down to the image."

But Nebuchadnezzar had the music play again. They didn't bow down. The king got mad. He said, "Poke up the fire good. Grab these men." And they tied them with their hats on their heads and their court garments on—they were rulers, you know—and pitched them in the fire. The fire was so hot when they were put in that it killed those strong soldiers who put them in. But all the fire did to Shadrach, Meshach, and Abednego was to burn their bands off, and they walked around in the fire. And One came and walked with them, and His form was one like the Son of man. I think Nebuchadnezzar was converted right there. The proclamation he gave showed he believed in the true God.

They did not have to count the cost. They had already counted it and considered whether it pays to serve God or not.

Brave Daniel, Too, Served God Faithfully When Threatened With the Lion's Den

There is the case of Daniel. They made a decree that nobody should pray to any god for thirty days and have the king above everybody, that nobody could serve any other gods or pray to anybody else for thirty days. And "now when Daniel knew that the writing was signed, he went into his house: and his windows being open in his chamber toward Jerusalem, he kneeled upon his knees three times a day, and prayed, and gave thanks before his God, as he did aforetime" (Dan. 6:10).

Now Daniel knew just what they did, and it didn't make a tremor in his voice when he prayed. It didn't make him hesitate and say, "O, God, give me courage." He had already made up his mind to that, and he opened the window. He didn't pray in the secret closet this time. (There are times to pray in secret, and there are times to pray in public.) He opened his window and prayed toward the God of Jerusalem as he had done before, three times a day. I say, he served God without regard to the consequences, without taking thought for what would happen! Daniel already knew God was greater than a den of lions.

Let me tell you, my friends, what happens isn't your business. That is God's business. Your business is to serve God day by day, and risk yourself with Him and let God do the rest.

Peter and John Obeyed God Rather Than Men, Took Beating and Shame Without Care

It is the same way in the New Testament. In the fourth chapter of Acts there was a time of testing.

"But Peter and John answered and said unto them, Whether it

be right in the sight of God to hearken unto you more than unto God, judge ye. For we cannot but speak the things which we have seen and heard. So when they had further threatened them, they let them go, finding nothing how they might punish them, because of the people: for all men glorified God for that which was done."—Acts 4:19-21.

And in the fifth chapter they were arrested again. Now listen:

"And when they had brought them, they set them before the council: and the high priest asked them, Saying, Did not we straitly command you that ye should not teach in this name? and, behold, ye have filled Jerusalem with your doctrine, and intend to bring this man's blood upon us. Then Peter and the other apostles answered and said, We ought to obey God rather than men."

We ought to obey God rather than man! That settled it. If God said so, that settled it. Wouldn't you like this Christmas to say, "I will, one time, give God a gift and not renege on God. I will not be an Indian giver. I won't take it back"? Make God a gift of yourself, lock, stock, and barrel, and don't take it back tomorrow.

Make Your Decision Permanent: Do Not Take It Back!

Jews had a way, commanded in the Old Testament, that if a man had a Jewish slave, after seven years he could set him free. At the end of that time every Jewish slave owned by a Jew was set free. Here is a wife. She has only been a slave a year or two. It is not time to set her free. Her children were born in slavery, it is not time to set them free. Suppose a man said, "I love my master and wife; I am not going to leave, but will be your slave." He says, "I would rather stay here and be your slave." And he brings him to the doorpost, and the servant puts his ear to the post and his master takes an awl and pushes it through and makes a hole in his ear, and then he is a slave forever. Read Exodus 21:1-6.

In Bible times it was a custom among these Hebrews who had Jewish slaves, if the slave were willing to go on and be a slave forever, to put an awl hole through his ear. Wouldn't you like to say, "O God, take me to the doorpost and put a hole through my ear—not just until I get a better job, not just until I find a job that I think will turn out better, but let me be Yours. Put an awl through my ear. Make me Yours from here on out"? Wouldn't you like to have that settled?

Let me tell a story. I have told it before, but I want to tell it again.

When I was a ten-year-old boy we lived on a ranch in West Texas, and Christmas time to us was wonderful. For instance, we got an orange at Christmas. We very rarely had any at any other time in the year. We would get twisted candy and a few nuts, and we had a good time. It didn't take much to make a happy Christmas. Every one got an orange. We didn't have orange groves in Texas then. They all came from California, and were rather expensive, and we were poor. I wonder how many people remember when you didn't get an orange except at Christmas? (Many held hands.) So at Christmas we each got an orange.

My stepmother said, "Now, children, I can make a fruit cake and I will have to make the citron with the orange peelings. I will candy the orange peelings if you will give yours to me."

So every one agreed. That may seem a little funny to you. Why should children object to giving the orange peel? But if you got just one a year, you could eat the peel with a little sugar and it was delicious, and we hadn't had an orange since last Christmas. We used to get bananas and we not only ate the bananas, but we scraped all the inside of the peeling. You don't do that now. Yes, the orange peel is really wonderfully good with sugar. Now my stepmother said that if we would give her the orange peelings she would make a cake.

We agreed, and she put the orange peels up on top of the kitchen safe. We didn't have any refrigerator, of course. It was a safe with tin doors and nail holes punched in the doors. So she put the peelings up on top of that so we couldn't see them. They were to be left there several days, then Mother was going to candy them. I got to thinking about the orange peels. That orange was given to me for Christmas and I didn't have to give it, did I? Why did I give it all? I ought to have kept a little bit, one good section. I could have eaten it with some sugar. I thought, "Well, I don't think she needs that much," so I went back, reached high on the safe and got one piece of the orange peeling and ate it with some sugar. Boy, it was good!

A day or two later as I thought about it I decided I could have one more piece. It was mine anyway, wasn't it? So I took another section from the top of the safe. You know, I lost count of how many times I went back. One day when I reached up there for one piece of *my* orange peeling there wasn't anybody's up there!

And you know, I have told God many times, "Lord, you can have me. Take me anywhere you want me to go. I will give up anything in this world. You deserve it and You can have it." I have said that and meant it; but the first thing I knew, I felt myself reaching back on top of the safe to take myself back and have my own way instead of God's way. I was an "Indian giver."

Would't you like, as this Christmas season comes on, to say, "God helping me, I will commit myself to God to be a bondslave to Jesus Christ from now on, and I will take no thought for the morrow nor worry today what I will have to eat"?

Somebody says, "Brother Rice, I would like to tithe, but I have so many bills to pay." Can you never think about God without thinking about bills at the same time?

Somebody says, "God has called me, but if I go, I will have to leave my family." Can you never think about God without thinking about your family, too?

The wise men would never have

come from the East if they had thought about their families. The shepherds never would have left their sheep if they couldn't think about the Baby Jesus without thinking about sheep. Some Christians never get their minds on God enough to forget sheep. Some Christians never get their minds on God enough to forget what they eat. That is the reason Jesus said to the disciples in the fourth chapter of John, "Lift up your eyes, and look on the fields; for they are white already to harvest" —"Get your eyes off this food and look on the poor lost souls." Oh, if you would ever get your mind on God enough to forget other things! *Take no thought!*

If somebody wants you to be a Sunday School teacher, you say, "If I teach I will have to give up this and that and the other and be here on time." Can't you do all that for God? Couldn't you ever count the cost and make up your mind and come to this conclusion that when God said do a thing, you don't have to stop and consider it anew?

Can You Not Trust God Blindly Without Seeing Where the Road May Lead?

A certain horse my father used to have is a great lesson to me. This horse was blind. You could get on him and ride him and other people couldn't tell the difference. You could hardly tell it yourself. He was blind, but you could ride down the road and this horse couldn't see a place he put his foot before him, yet he trusted the man riding him and he went right ahead.

The truth of the matter is, the way my daddy got him, he traded for him a horse that had the heaves. He rode beside a fellow one night and this horse had such a wonderful gait my father said, "What about trading horses?"

"All right, I will trade with you."

My dad said, "No questions asked and we will trade for good?"

This fellow said, "All right," and he got down and they changed saddles and my father got on this blind horse and rode him home that night. The next day my dad discovered he had traded for a blind horse, but a horse that trusted his rider.

My friend, listen to me, wouldn't you like to be able to say, "O God, I can serve you blind"?

Oh, friend, if God comes to borrow $1.00 from you, would you ask Him to sign a promissory note? We ought not to. If God wanted to buy something from you on credit, would you look up and see if His credit was good? Brother Nicholas, if a man comes and wants to buy from you on credit, you would ask Mr. Patton about it or you would look up his name in Dunn and Bradstreet. How many of you have to weigh the thing out and check up on God before you say yes or no to Him!

Wouldn't it be wonderful if we Christians could learn to act without any fear of the consquences, without considering the consequences? That is what the Bible says, "Take no thought for the morrow. Take no thought for your body. Take no thought for your life. Take no thought for what you will eat or drink."

Wouldn't it be wonderful if the money you put in the collection on Sunday was just put in without any regard for what you would need next week? Isn't that right? I would find out what God says to do, then do it without thinking about that bill that has to be paid this week. Wouldn't that be the right way?

If God says, "John, I want you to go to Africa," wouldn't it be right for me to say, "All right, Lord, I will go"? First, should I sit down and say, "There is my wife. She will not want to leave her mother and dad. They are old. They live up here in Cooke County. The other children are gone. They love her, and she may never see them again"? Would it be right to stop and consider and say, "Wait, Lord. Let me check up on this business before I say yes. Shall I take my children into blackest Africa, away from schools, away from their companions, and let them live in a hut with thatched roof, with a dirt floor, and wild beasts howling in the back yard at night? Would it be right? What am I going to do if God says go to Africa? Before I say yes to God, do I always have to take up the whole thing every time and find out whether it pays to serve Him, find out whether it is worthwhile to do what He says?

Here is a thing every Christian ought to get settled: "I will count the cost once and for all and find out if it pays to serve God. And when I have found that out, I will have it settled. I will say yes to God. If God says to me, "Do so and so," I will say, "All right, I will go," without taking thought except to find the will of God.

Do you know why people these days don't have steam automobiles? Steam automobiles are a good deal cheaper to run than gas automobiles. They used to have a good many steam cars. Some things about them are better. One thing, you don't have to have any gear shift. For years experimenters have spent thousands of dollars trying to make an automobile without a gear shift. A steam engine automatically adjusts to any load and never stalls. The more power, the less speed and the less power, the more speed. Why don't all people use steam cars, and why don't they make them? *Because it takes ten minutes to get the water hot!* and you can't always wait that long. So steam cars are now museum specimens.

God wants somebody here to serve Him, but He has always got to wait for you to get the steam hot when He wants you to do anything! Do you think God is going to always, always wait for you to take thought for every thing else, when He says, "Go"?

What about this kind of Christian who every time God brings up a duty, there is a big tussle and knock-down, drag-out fight before He can get you to do anything, while you again decide whether you are going to serve God, while you count the cost again! Do you always have to count the cost anew and see what it is going to cost you before you decide whether you are going to do what God said?

My brother Joe had a model T Ford. He told me he always knew how to start it: "Any time you jack up both hind wheels and crank it until the water boils, it will start."

If you go at it that way, you can get some Christians to teach a Sunday School class. You can get them to tithe, or get them to come to prayer meeting, or get them to testify. If you really jack both hind wheels up and crank until the water boils, you can get them to do something for God. Is God content with the kind of service that comes always with a grudge, always with the brakes on?

I was in a revival meeting down in southwest Texas. I went to Hico, near Lampasas. They have live oak trees and white limestone everywhere. I was in a hurry. I went in my car. I was going back to the revival, and I came to a fellow whose car was out of gas, or something was wrong with his car. I tried to help get his car started, but I couldn't. So I told him, "If you want me to, I will pull you in." I hooked on with a tow chain. Over those rough, rocky roads we went, driving about thirty miles an hour. The man in the car behind me couldn't see. He sat back there and kept putting on the brakes. Finally I stopped to see what was the matter. He said, "I will just sit here if you don't mind. Just unhook the chain and I will send my boy after the car later."

Do you think God wants to take you anywhere when He always has to drag you? When you always have the brakes on? When you won't go unless you can see the road? You are always thinking about what it will cost. "Will I have something to eat? I would serve You, Lord, but my family may starve." I would sing in the choir but I don't think it is worth it." I would teach a Sunday School class, but I would have to study, and I would have to give up going to see Mother every second Sunday." Why don't you say, "I will make up my mind like the shepherds who didn't care about the sheep when the Saviour was born, like the wise men from the East who left home and families and brought their money to this far country to see Him and gave all they had and went home." Wouldn't you like to say, as did Mary, "Be it unto me according to thy word." *Never mind what it will cost.* It will cost you plenty, *but never mind!* And like Joseph who, when he arose out of his sleep, went and took Mary home with him. Why don't you say, "I will count the cost no more. You can have all I have. I will lay it on the altar and not take it back." Wouldn't you like to say that today? I would like to, wouldn't you?

I wonder who is here today who is not a Christian but you want to be. Can you say at this Christmas season, "I will trust Him to be my Saviour. I will take Him as mine. God loves me, offered me the best Gift in the world—His Son—and I will take Him today"? Will you come and take Christ as your Saviour?

(Three claimed Christ as Saviour.)

The Blessings of Trouble

(As preached Sunday night, June 21, 1959, at
Calvary Baptist Church, Wheaton, Illinois, recorded.)

"God is our refuge and strength, a very present help in trouble.—Ps. 46:1.

Trouble is a common lot of all men and women everywhere. I want you to think about it because you are going to have trouble. You may not think so now, but you will. Job said in Job 14:1 that "man that is born of a woman is of few days, and full of trouble." Again Job 5:7 says, "Yet man is born unto trouble, as the sparks fly upward."

It is natural to have trouble. It is a part of humanity to have trouble. We had just as well get ready for trouble. Troubles come on the whole race. There are many reasons why we should expect trouble all down through the years and should be prepared for it. God has the answer for trouble.

Recently a number of things came to my mind. I had such blessings as I waited on God, and He seemed to tell me that I ought to remind others of the blessings in trouble.

For some period of time, perhaps two or three years, I who have long years been fighting for evangelism and trying to bring back (and God has blessed and helped bring back) mass evangelism in America, have had to take a stand against modernism and yoking up with unbelievers and compromising in order to get a crowd. I have taken a stand and so the popular winds now blow with the big popular crowd and the newspaper notoriety and compromise, and my position has not been popular. I have lost subscribers to THE SWORD, I have had lots of abusive letters. The other day in one day's mail, I had three photostatic copies of three different letters written by three different men in the Billy Graham organization, all of them full-time letter writers and all of them saying mean things about me—how I was old and jealous, how I refused to preach to modernists these days like some others did, etc. Never mind about that except that since the same pattern comes in so many hundreds of other letters, we know that people follow the pattern that is being set.

And then sometime back when some good friends left the board of THE SWORD OF THE LORD for one cause and another, I had good reason to study—what does God mean and what ought I to do about it, and what ought to be the Christian's attitude toward trouble. Whether it is trouble in the flesh, trouble from sickness, trouble from age, disease, from proverty, loneliness or from persecution, what ought a Christian's attitude be about trouble?

I find God talking to my heart through the Word, and I trust that God will talk to you also. The Bible, then, has the answer to trouble. I am glad. Thank God, you can go to the Bible and find what to do in any kind of a situation and God has the answer about trouble.

I. Trouble Comes From God

First, trouble comes from God. Let's say that again! Trouble comes from God, either directly in the best will of God, or indirectly because God allows it after consideration, after weighing it and deciding. Nobody ever has trouble but that God considered it and decided to let you have trouble. Trouble is from God!

1. The Universal Trouble Inherent in Mankind Is From God

That is evident from several lines of thought. First, the trouble that the whole flesh is heir to, the whole human race, was appointed and was determined and is the sentence of God on the human race.

When Adam and Eve sinned in the garden, God said to the man, "Cursed is the ground for thy sake . . . Thorns also and thistles shall it bring forth to thee . . . In the sweat of thy face shalt thou eat bread" (Gen. 3:17, 18, 19). You see, all the trouble in nature—the plagues, insect pests, disease of crops, all the droughts, all the floods—these things come because of the intentional curse of God on the earth and on men. God said, "I am determined you are going to work for your living. I am determined you are going to have to chop briars and dig up stumps and fight mosquitoes and you are going to have disease germs; you are going to have trouble." That is part of the lot of the whole human race which God plainly ordained and which He said that He had commanded. So man shall have trouble.

To the woman God said, "I will greatly multiply thy sorrow and thy conception; in sorrow thou shalt bring forth children; and thy desire shall be to thy husband, and he shall rule over thee" (Gen. 3:16). "In sorrow thou shalt bring forth children." All the pain of childbirth, all the long months, the morning sickness, the whims, the discomfort, the misunderstandings, and the nervous periods which are part of a woman's life that are more or less normal and expected among women, God intended and planned.

I do not mean that a man

should fret about having to work for a living, nor that sickness ought to make people unhappy. I do not mean that a woman ought not to be a good wife and good friend and good mother in time of childbearing. I just mean that the discomfort and the trouble are a part of the curse on the whole human race. God sends trouble; it is meant for good and comes from God. So the Bible clearly says.

There are certain things that follow then inevitably. The way God made us and the earth where God put us and the surroundings that God has prepared for us: there are certain things there. In the first place, you are going to have to work and that means sometimes you will be tired. Sometimes you will have to work when you don't feel like working. People have said to me, "How do you go without vacation? How do you go summer and winter? How do you work six, seven days a week?" I don't deserve credit for it. Most of my life I have done what I wanted to do. I mean I have delighted in preaching. It has been pleasure; it has been joy. I have often thought, Doesn't it seem strange that a fellow would preach the Gospel and have as good a time as I have and get paid for it to get to preach the Gospel, when I would be so glad to preach if I had to dig ditches to make a living and preach too? But I say, most of the time I have been glad, but you had just as well face it, there come times when one doesn't have the strength he once had and he still needs to work. You are going to be tired and you will still need to work.

Often, when other men were tired, I was not. I have had unusual vitality. God has wonderfully cared for my body. In the first place, I was strong and husky as a young fellow. I never drank nor smoked nor indulged in some of the dissipations which make others weak. Then I had a naturally good constitution by the blessing of God. But there comes a time when you are weary, and you still need to work. There comes a time when you had rather rest, but you need to work. Then there comes a time when your hair gets gray—or gets lost. And there comes a time when your teeth decay or fall out. There comes a time when your bones get brittle, etc. Natural trouble is a part of the plan of God.

And with that then come disease and pain: God made this body to suffer pain. Why would there be so many nerve endings that make pain? God evidently meant some good out of pain and trouble. It is a part of God's dealing with man.

2. This World Is Planned So There Must Be Separations, Partings

I say trouble is from God. In the nature of the case, being frail and human as we are, there must come separation from those we love. It is strange that people we love have to be gone so far, and some of them, so far we never, never see them. I have been with many good pastors in revival campaigns, and we have had blessed, sweet fellowship. Oh, we have longed to see one another, but our paths don't cross very often and so we do not often have the comfort of each other's company. But that is part of the plan of God. I say trouble is ours.

And separation—I thought this week about my daughter Elizabeth, and son-in-law, Walt Handford, who have just taken over another baby. God willing, as soon as things can be arranged, they will have the adoption papers signed and all fixed up, and that will mean four babies they have adopted. I thought with a little bit of a catch in my heart and a little bit of, will you say, presentiment? No, maybe rather just a little bit of knowing in the future what others don't know.

You know the Lord said, 'Yes, go ahead and marry, you will have trouble in the flesh.' Paul said, "But I spare you." You needn't tell any young people with moonlight in their eyes and all the chimes sounding and the bells ringing and the flowers smelling and the birds singing—why, you needn't tell young people about it, but their marriage and family and children mean trouble! All those little ones—that means lots of times Libby is going to be up in the night when she wishes she could sleep. After awhile they may turn out to be the best in the world, or they may not; children sometimes bring many a heartbreak by their sins, but if they turn out to be the best in the world, they will still go another way one of these times. And the two boys she thinks so much of, one day she will be shocked to find they think more of some little flip of a girl than they do of her, some girl who doesn't have as much sense as Libby. The wise mother who loves them and sacrificed and prayed and wept over them, will be ignored when they go off after somebody else. And the girls will be the same way.

I was thinking a bit ago about the night Chuck and Mary Lloys married. We came back to the living room after they had gotten away. After changing to traveling clothes and the tossing of the bride's bouquet and the good-byes, one of the other girls came and said, "Mother, I will put away Mary Lloys' things." And Mrs. Rice said, "No, you won't! You leave them alone! Mary said I could put them away." And Mrs. Rice began to sob. I said, "Now Mother, Mary Lloys is happy and you must be happy. Never mind, don't be crying." She said, "You don't care! She is out and gone and you don't care!"

I said, "When I first held this baby in my arms, held her very close and saw how black and dark was her hair, and how round and chubby her face," I said, "From that hour to this I have known it was coming, that sometime somebody would come along, maybe riding a white charger, and maybe just a boy working his way through school, and she is going to fall for him. This good-by I thought of a long time ago and shed my tears about it."

I am saying that God planned separation, pain, disease, old age, failure, disappointments, loss of friends and after awhile death. That is in the will of God for people—we had just as well face it. Trouble is from God.

3. God Intended That Good People Should Suffer Persecution

All the saints of God, the best men in the Bible, the best people since Bible times, have suffered.

There was Joseph, a noble man. There are only two or three men in the Bible to whom much space is given about which not a word of criticism is given. One of those is Joseph; another is Daniel. Yet strangely enough, Joseph suffered much. He was sold as a slave by his own brothers, a teen-age boy taken off despite his cries and pleading, not even allowed to see his dad. And they persuaded his dad he had been killed by a wild beast. They tore off his garment of many colors and sold him as a slave down to Egypt in a strange country.

He served in the house of Potiphar, the captain of the guard. Then a wicked woman set her eyes on him and when she couldn't seduce him into sin, she slandered him, and lied on him and got him put in jail. Poor Joseph, a homesick country boy, in the big city in a far-off country, slandered and abused, nobody to stand up for him, no friends to say that he had been honest and straight. And kept in jail!

After awhile two men, the king's butler and the king's baker, had dreams and God revealed them to him and he told them. Then later when the butler was delivered, he told him, "I will tell Pharoah about you; I will get you out of here," but he forgot it and two full years went by. His brothers forsook him and hated him, sold him into slavery. He was slandered by a wicked woman, spent years in jail in the midst of his youth. You know God's good people suffer; the saints of God suffer.

I mentioned Daniel. Daniel was carried into captivity when only a boy, only a child. "Children," the Bible says. I suppose he was a youngster, of high school age, carried into captivity. And he lived right and good, and God was with him. He was cast into the lions' den, his life was threatened again and again, with everything at stake, hated and abused.

And Jeremiah stood up for God and got publicly slapped and beaten and then put in a dungeon. Then he was put down in the mud pit where the mud came up half way to his waist, and was saved by an Ethiopian man who pulled him out. They finally carried him into captivity with the remnant left after the Babylonian captivity and he went down to Egypt. Poor old Jeremiah, a saint of God! He said, "Oh that my head were waters, and mine eyes a fountain of tears, that I might weep day and night for the slain of the daughter of my people!" (Jer. 9:1). Jeremiah, the weeping prophet!

God's saints suffered. They ought to suffer. Suffering is from God. That is the way it ought to be.

You know how John the Baptist suffered. He was hated and despised and finally put in jail because he had preached against sin. Then he had his head cut off because a wicked woman didn't like him.

And there was Paul the apostle—stoned and left for dead, dragged out of town like a dead horse. Paul fought the lions at Ephesus, was put in jail in Rome and had a chain on his hands; finally had his head cut off. Other saints of God suffered. That is the way it ought to be.

Suffering is from God. Good people ought to remember then that suffering comes to saints of God.

Listen to this Scripture and note the attitude a Christian ought to have and what a Christian ought to accept as a fact. In II Corinthians 4:8-12, we read, "We are troubled on every side, yet not distressed . . . ." (Trouble but the remedy for trouble, yes, trouble, but comfort from God.) "We are troubled on every side, yet not distressed; we are perplexed, but not in despair; Persecuted, but not forsaken; cast down, but not destroyed; Always bearing about in the body the dying of the Lord Jesus, that the life also of Jesus might be made manifest in our body. For we which live are alway delivered unto death for Jesus' sake, that the life also of Jesus might be made manifest in our mortal flesh. So then death worketh in us, but life in you."

The Christian is expected to have trouble. And then trouble is not outside the will of God. Trouble may be in the will of God. It is always permitted by God. It may be the highest and best time God ever gave you when you had trouble. Trouble is from God.

4. But God in Love Permits Trouble Only As It Is Good

I say, then, only as God permits it, only as God in loving kindness plans it and permits it, does trouble ever come.

We ought to remember Job. The Bible reminds us to consider the end of Job "that the Lord is very pitiful, and of tender mercy" (Jas. 5:11). We ought not only to think how he suffered—terrible suffering—but how God delivered him and rewarded him and how the suffering was for good.

The Devil came one day to talk to God, and God said, "See my servant Job? He serves me righteously and gives offerings and prays for his children. See my servant Job?"

The Devil said, "If you would let me put my hands on him, I would show you he won't serve you anymore."

The Lord said, "Go ahead, but don't touch his body."

Well, the Devil took away Job's possessions by the plan of God, killed all of his children by the plain permission of God, but he couldn't touch Job's body. The Devil came back whining and complaining, "You have put a hedge around him; you won't let me to him. If you would let me get my hands on his body, he would curse you and die; he would quit you."

God said, "Go ahead, but spare his life. I have a hedge about him but you may reach your hand through the hedge."

So boils broke out and Job scraped the scabs and dirt from his body and worms off his body with a bit of potsherd. His servants sneered at him. His wife said, "Why don't you curse God and die?" The three best friends he had in the world came to "comfort" him, and said, "Yes, you have been in some devilment. This wouldn't have come to you if you had lived right." So Job prayed to die!

Listen, that all came because God planned it and permitted it to His own glory! But God restored Job's health and gave him seven sons and three daughters again and great wealth and riches. And millions of us have been blessed by Job's suffering. Thank God, 'the end of the Lord is pitiful and of tender mercy.'

I say the Devil can only go as far as he is allowed. Even when Satan means it for evil, God means trouble for good. He did with Paul: "a thorn in the flesh, that messenger of Satan to buffet me," Paul said. Even when Satan means it for evil, the Devil can only go as far as God lets him. And God always uses it to His own glory. 'He makes the wrath of men to praise Him.' He makes the shenanigans of the Devil to praise Him, too, and to bless His children. Thank God, "All things work together for good to them that love God" (Rom. 8:28). "All things"—not a part of them—"All things work together for good to them that love God." Nothing can happen to a saint of God but by the loving, careful decision of One who loves him so much He gave His Son to die for him.

Yes, trouble is from God. It is not bad, but good when God allows it. And we ought to have a heart to believe it. The good hand of God brings trouble—tears as well as laughter, sickness as well as health, poverty as well as prosperity. Remember that good things like trouble come from God.

II. There Is Real Blessing In Trouble

Second, there is blessing to trouble. You say the *trials?* No, I said the *blessings*. The *blessings* of trouble. Does that seem to be a contradiction? No. Remember the Lord Jesus said, "Blessed are they that mourn" (Matt. 5:4). What is it? It is blessed to mourn. Oh, the rich seed when tears of a Christian fall into the ground. What wonderful crops they produce! Oh, the beautiful flowers that come in the flower beds of affliction. Oh, the sweet balm that comes to the Christian who is lonely in the night of sorrow. Trouble is good. "Blessed are they that mourn: for they shall be comforted," the Lord Jesus says (Matt. 5:4).

Then let us say there are certain blessings of trouble. What are the blessings of trouble?

1. The Blessing of Correction for Sin

First, there is correction. You know one ought to want to do right! In my revival campaign at Cleveland, Ohio, among the hundreds saved was a pastor's son. He got under such conviction. His mother and dad didn't know whether he was old enough or not, but he raised Cain until he got saved. On the road home he said, "Mama, you are going to have to help me be good. When I do anything wrong, whip me hard, Mama, because I have got to be good." He wanted to be good. It is not bad to get a whipping when it makes you a good boy.

I was thinking a bit ago of what happened in Amarillo, Texas, after I had preached to a full tabernacle of people one night with great blessing. In the Capital Hotel that night a man called the room where I was with three other preachers, and he said, "I need somebody to pray for me." He came to the room, this young man, but a drunkard, a confirmed alcoholic. He made twenty-six thousand dollars the year before selling life insurance. His wife had quit him. He was already a drunkard, already in such despair that he had tried to kill himself three times.

And he came down for us to pray for him, this fellow who had been drinking some, and he said to one of the preachers, "Here, hold this," and he handed his lighted cigarette to one of the preachers. The preacher held it. I could hardly keep from laughing even at that most tragic time! He was embrassed, but the fellow didn't think anything of it.

This is what that drunkard prayed: "O God, make me a good boy like my mama wanted me to be." This drunken man, a man with lots of money, a man whose wife had quit him, a man who tried to commit suicide, said, "Lord, make me a good boy."

You know if after awhile there comes that cry of a heart that wants to be good, if God does some of that in suffering, that is good, isn't it? That is not bad!

There is blessing in correction then! Listen, a child one day will rise up to call blessed the hoary head of a dad or a mother who whipped him and made him mind.

I talked to a good woman at McComb, Mississippi, a southern gentlewoman and aristocrat and a Christian lady, a lovely southern gentlewoman in the best southern tradition! She told me once (and she laughed and cried too while she told it) how when she was to get married and her mother was fitting her wedding dress, she complained, and 'didn't like this,' and 'it took so long.' Finally her mother said, "Young lady, take that off! You may be old enough to get married, but you are not old enough to sass your mother and get by with it. Take it off!" She took off the wedding dress and her mother whipped her good. After that she fitted the dress without any more remarks. She laughed and cried while she told it to me later. She thanked God for that kind of a mother!

If God wants to whip you, He has some good reason and it will turn out good. Thank God for any sin corrected.

Would you thank God for the doctor who cut out a cancer and saved your life? I saw a little girl this morning with a cast on her arm. Two days ago she broke her arm. There is some pain, but wouldn't you thank God for a doctor who set those bones, broken in two places, and put them in a good cast? You wouldn't say the doctor is mean, would you? Neither is it bad when God corrects His child! We should thank God.

How often a child, rebellious and mean, won't sleep and raises the whole household until a good spanking makes the child give up and he has sweet peace. Then, how he loves Dad and Mother.

Thank God for correction, for trouble that brings people to their senses, to weigh their thoughts and deeds and judge them in the light of the Word of God for correction.

2. Trouble Often Leads to Restored Fellowship

For another thing, we can thank God for restoration of fellowship! Isn't it good when God kisses away your tears? When God takes a prodigal son in His arms and calls for the robe of righteousness and brings shoes for his feet and they kill the fatted calf, when the prodigal comes home? Trouble is a home-coming. So often fellowship is thus restored with God and it is sweet. If it takes trouble to have fellowship, if it takes chastising to have the sweet consciousness of God's presence, then thank God for trouble. It is always good when God has His way.

In Dallas, Texas, years ago, I was sick for ten days with flu and a very high fever. There were some days of pain and I was set apart from the work for awhile. One of my girls disobeyed again and again. Finally Mother said, "Daddy, she has done it again. She didn't obey me." So I said, "Go get my belt." She brought me the belt and when I began to whip the child she said, "Daddy, I am sorry! I am sorry, Daddy!" I stopped and said, "Yes, but you weren't sorry until the punishment came." Then I talked some more and whipped some more and my heart bled. She said, "I am sorry. I will do right now." She went back to her housework.

As I lay there on the bed I thought, "Lord, I don't know why these ten days laid aside, but don't stop till the job is done. Lord, whatever You plan, make me to know it. Don't stop till the job is done. Whatever You start to do, do it, Lord, and get it fixed." It is not bad to have punishment or trouble if it causes you to be right with God and restoration of fellowship. So we can thank God!

3. Suffering May Help Grow Strong Character

Here is another thing. There is blessing in trouble because of what it does to character. People are never very strong Christians who never suffer. No man has very much conviction and character until he suffers some. "Sweet are the uses of adversity," Shakespeare said, "which, like the venomous toad, hath yet a precious jewel in his head." Yes, thank God for trouble. "Blessed are they that mourn" (Matt. 5:4).

There is real character in trouble. Those who have suffered have gained patience. "Tribulation worketh patience, and patience, experience; and experience, hope"; so if you want to grow in character, don't shun the hard places (Rom. 5:3, 4).

Some things I have learned from being poor. I am glad I have had to work hard. That did something for me. I thank God also for a lot of other pains and troubles for God has meant them for good.

My mother went to be with the Lord before I was six years old, and I have always missed her. She was a sweet and dear woman, and, many people have told me, one of the smartest and one of the best women they ever knew I believe it. Perhaps a boy ought to think that of his mother anyhow. After my mother died, for years I felt a little resentful. I needed a mother. I grew up in wild West Texas country where we didn't have much church, didn't have much Christian influence. They were a wild, drinking, cursing lot and one could not be very particular when one picked his class because they were little communities and scattered. But later on God put His hand on me to preach and I began to see why. Here is something a lot of people don't understand. I love poor people. I understand poor working people, and people in sorrow. I may not feel at home with the high and mighty, the big cars and the fine houses, but I understand people in trouble. I have had sorrow, too. I know how to "weep with those that weep."

I suppose that is one reason why, when I was in Dallas and had a daily radio program, thousands looked to me as a pastor and called on me in trouble, called on me about a job or about relief or when their loved ones died. I had funerals all over Dallas, for people who heard me on the radio and kept up with me, though they were not members of my church. Because I found the comfort of God, I learned to weep with those who weep, and to comfort those who need comfort.

I say there are blessings in trouble. We can thank God for that.

4. Trouble Often Brings Blessed Comfort From God and From Friends

Trouble may bring God's conscious nearness. You know, God can be near in trouble in the way He can't in better days. Have you a house full of friends, having a big time? You don't need God, do you? You don't need any money. You have plenty in the bank. You never know you need a friend until you are in real trouble. So you never know you need God, maybe, until some lonely time that friend leaves you, then you go to God. When the children are gone, or when you get old, or when you are misunderstood, or when you are in desperate need of something, you call, then you find God is near you, the fellowship of God in a way that you wouldn't have it otherwise.

Then the blessing of trouble is that you find who are your true friends. You never know true friends until they suffer with you. Many a friend turns out to be a fair-weather friend. Oh, yes, "I am all for you; you are wonderful." But wait until somebody else comes along and teaches a little different, then you are not so wonderful. Yes, fair-weather friends are soon 'gone. Paul said, "I know this, that after my departing shall grievous wolves enter in among you [preachers right here] not sparing the flock . . . to draw away disciples after them" (Acts 20:29, 30). Paul said, "All they which are in Asia be turned away from me" (II Tim. 1:15). But when people suffer with you, then you learn who your true friends are. You learn who will stand, and that is good. You learn some real friends by trouble. You never have that kind of friends unless you have trouble and need them and they prove themselves.

5. There Are Eternal Rewards for Suffering

Another thing, when you suffer for Jesus' sake, there is an eternal reward. "For our light affliction, which is but for a moment, worketh for us a far more exceeding and eternal weight of glory" (II Cor. 4:17). Couldn't you suffer a little now so you can thank God for a thousand or a million years? Couldn't you suffer a little now and be misunderstood in order to live closer to Jesus in the kingdom age and have a cottage or palace somewhere close to the throne? There is a reward in Heaven.

And, "Blessed are ye, when men shall revile you, and persecute you, and shall say all manner of evil against you falsely,. for my sake. Rejoice, and be exceeding glad: for great is your reward in heaven" (Matt. 5:11, 12).

For all the tears you ever wept for a poor sinner who gets saved, you will have only glad laughter, and one day you will rise and shine "as the stars forever," with all the mourning, all the trouble for Jesus' sake, paid back.

III. What To Do About Trouble

Now, what should a Christian do about trouble? Trouble is to be expected; God sends trouble. There are blessings in trouble; so what should a Christian do about trouble.

1. Profit by Your God-Sent Trouble

In James 1:2-4 we have this blessed instruction about trouble:

"My brethren, count it all joy when ye fall into divers temptations; knowing this, that the trying of your faith worketh patience. But let patience have her perfect work, that ye may be perfect and entire, wanting nothing."

Let patience, in trouble, have her perfect work! First of all, take your medicine, by which I mean, find out if you did wrong, you earned it. Bill, did you ever get a good licking and say, "I didn't do anything." But you knew better? Well, you had just as well face it and acknowledge it if you did wrong. Maybe you had better check up and see if you did do something wrong. Maybe you needed a good licking. Then I would humble my heart; I would wait on God; I would find out what is wrong; I would take the medicine and say, "Lord, whatever You want to do with me, You do it and get this thing fixed up. If I am wrong, I want to get right." That is a proper attitude toward trouble. So humble your heart.

I have been thinking about this because of my troubles and constant abuse, and two or three things came very clear. One of them is: Don't be proud and haughty. Aren't you glad that God allows even trouble that you don't deserve, even accusations which are false, even misunderstandings, to make your heart tender and you cry to God? When you lose all of your friends when you don't deserve to lose them, you can still thank God. It can humble your heart and make you draw near to God. You can draw near to God better with a broken heart. You know what God wants? "The sacrifices of God are a broken spirit: a broken and a contrite heart, O God, thou wilt not despise" (Ps. 51:17). You had better have some grief because even if somebody stole all of your money, even if you got fired from a job unjustly, even if people lied on you and accused you of things that were not true, if it broke your heart, if it caused you to pray, if it caused you to humble yourself before God, that would be good, wouldn't it?

All right then, so take your medicine and let God work the good work, whatever is needed.

2. Be Sure You Submit Joyfully to God's Hand in Trouble

That means another thing: Submit yourself joyfully to the hand of God. When trouble comes, say, "This is from God. I am not going to fight it. I will not grow bitter. I am not going to worry nor fret about it. This is from God."

A woman wrote me the other day, "Brother Rice, I think I know what we ought to do about things that are obviously from God. But what about trouble that doesn't come from God, but from our own stupidity and from other people's wickedness?"

I wrote back, "Troubles that come from our own stupidity come from God. And trouble that comes from other people's sins comes from God." She was married to a man whom she felt was a pretty bad fellow. He didn't treat her right, etc. She blamed herself and said she was stupid and so she could pray to God about some things but not about this. But I wrote her, "Listen, that is the hand of God. The thorn in the flesh Paul had was from the Devil, but God meant it for good and God said, 'I am going to keep it there, Paul: I can use you better.'"

So a thorn in the flesh, even if it is a "messenger from Satan to buffet you," is good and from God. And I would say like Paul did, "All right, Lord, then I will glory in mine infirmity." I would just say, "All right, Lord, it is the right thing and I am going to be glad." But you ask—be glad for somebody to mistreat you? Yes, if God wants it, and rejoice in the blessing.

Somebody asks, "But suppose you did wrong." Well, suppose your sins or your own stupidity bring trouble? All right, confess the fault and sin but God still makes it true that all things work for good. Your own sin? Yes. Your own failures? Yes. Your own stupidity? Yes. The attacks of Satan? Yes. The failure of friends? Yes. "All things work together for good." God means it for good. You just wait till God's Univac—that big machine God runs that fits every piece of the universe in together—brings in all the pieces and adds up the sum, and you are going to find out it turns out for good for the people of God. "All things work together for good." That is right! Maybe it doesn't look good by itself.

Dr. Ironside loved southern biscuits, I guess because he lived up north among you Yankees and didn't get many of them. So when he came to my church in Dallas I took him out to chicken dinner, hot biscuits and cream gravy. Dr. Ironside said, "I am afraid I ought not to eat another one," but he would butter another biscuit and eat it, then he would say, "Listen, I am afraid this is a sin," but he would butter another biscuit and eat it. And Dr. Ironside said once, "Do you like lard?" Roy, did you ever taste just lard? "Well," he said, "You wouldn't like that." "Do you like dry flour?" No "Did you ever taste baking powder?" Bill, that tastes awful; baking powder does. He said, "Do you like that? Well, you just wait till God mixes them all up together and gets His biscuits in the oven and gets them to rise good, and brown good; when God gets His biscuits brown you are going to like them. You might not like the lard by itself, nor the baking powder by itself, nor the dry flour by itself, nor the salt by itself, but when God mixes them, "all things work together" in God's oven and turn out good biscuits. And so "all things work together for good."

Your own sins—confess them? Yes. Forsake them? Yes. The failure of others—they are attacks of Satan—never mind—God is going to turn them out for good. You can thank God that when God gets through they will all turn out for good. If you had done right that would have turned out better. But God overcomes sin to make a blessing.

So what to do about trouble? Accept it joyfully. Joyfully? Yes. First of all, if you are persecuted for Jesus' sake, take it joyfully. Paul said, "Ye . . . took joyfully the spoiling of your goods" (Heb. 10:34). Ye took it joyfully.

And in Romans 5:3, ". . . We glory in tribulations also: knowing that tribulation worketh patience." The Bible doesn't say just be *resigned* to tribulation but *glory* in it.

And again the Lord said, "Blessed are ye, when men shall revile you, and persecute you, and shall say all manner of evil against you falsely, for my sake. Rejoice, and be exceeding glad: for great is your reward in heaven" (Matt. 5:11, 12).

So then face it and submit to the good hand of God joyfully.

3. Confess and Forsake Any Known Sin, When Trouble Comes

What to do about trouble? Confess and forsake any known sin! You say, "I don't know anything wrong." Well, it would be a mighty good time to check up, wouldn't it?

If somebody comes in to see the doctor and there is a great rash, a breaking out in the skin and the doctor says, "This is some kind of an allergy. What is wrong with you? I don't know." Well, the doctor puts on some kind of a salve and it doesn't do any good. "Well, this is some kind of an allergy. What is it?" And so they take tests—let's see—with one man I knew it was flour. He couldn't eat any bread or any gravy with flour. He couldn't have fried chicken dipped in flour. Isn't that strange, wheat flour made him violently sick?

There was another fellow who had a pet cat and he was allergic to the cat's fur and it would make him sick. That is strange, but literally, physically true. And to somebody else it is a little of this and a little of that. Some people can't eat pork; it makes them sick. And to somebody else, it is a certain kind of this or that and the other. Strawberries make some people sick—they have an allergy for strawberries. Isn't that strange? And they break out violently.

Well, now listen, what you had better do if you find you have got something wrong, you had better get the doctor and check up and find out what is wrong, hadn't you? Examine your heart. If you are going to take the Lord's Supper, "let a man examine himself, and so let him eat" (I Cor. 11:28). "If we would judge ourselves, we should not be judged," the Bible says (I Cor. 11:31). So then the thing for a Christian to do in trouble is to say, "I am going to find out anything that displeases God. I will confess and forsake anything God will help me find; I will dig it out." That would be a good thing, wouldn't it?

right, let's see (you people up here don't know about it), but did anybody ever live in poor people's homes and sometimes you got to smelling something bad? Well, what is it? It is a dead rat somewhere! Under the bed? No. Back of the stove? No. Where is it? In the closet? No. "Well, I put out some poison a week ago" but—*good night,* you find you have to dig into the wall and inside the partition there maybe you find a dead rat! Now these days they have got a different kind of poison, but the kind they used to have the rats would run off somewhere and crawl in a hole and die. I am just saying if you smell a rat" you had better dig it out, hadn't you?

Is any sin in the way? Ask God to help you find it! That is a good thing to do in trouble, isn't it?

4. Pray for Those Who Cause You Trouble

What else then? When you are in trouble, pray for anybody who causes you trouble. I have had a very sweet time recently. Two or three things I have added to my prayer list. One pastor out in California invited me (I didn't ask to go), and then—I won't go into the matter by which he humiliated me. Never mind—but I preached the Gospel and had somebody saved, etc. But you know what I did? I began to pray regularly for him. I got a letter the other day, an abusive letter, from a man who ought to know better. And so I just began pretty regularly to pray for him several times a day. You know what to do? "Pray for them that despitefully use you and persecute you." Return good for evil and pray for them that despitefully use you and persecute you. Pray for them; that is the way out.

And the Scripture says that you are to forgive people and return good for evil and thus you pour coals of fire on their head.

A woman came to a preacher one time and said, "My husband, he just runs me crazy, he is so mean to me, etc." And so the pastor said, "Have you ever tried what the Bible says about pouring coals of fire on his head?" She said, "No, I have scalded him with hot water, though." Well, the preacher said, "That wasn't what God meant." No, pray for them that misuse you.

Anybody causes you trouble? Why, take it to God in prayer; pray God to bless them; pray for good to happen!

5. Take Your Trouble to God In Prayer

What else should we do when trouble comes? Ah, pray! "And call upon me in the day of trouble: I will deliver thee, and thou shalt glorify me" (Ps. 50:15). And in Psalm 55:22 David said, "Cast thy burden upon the Lord, and he shall sustain thee."

In I Peter 5:7, "Casting all your care upon him; for he careth for you."

In Psalm 34:6 the psalmist said, "This poor man cried, and the Lord heard him, and saved him out of all his troubles." That is a good thing!

What are you going to do with trouble? Pray, keep on praying! Just pray and keep on praying. Pray God to have His perfect work and pray God to lead you. If you mourn, pray for God to comfort you and He will. So you can be "cast down but not destroyed;" "troubled on every side yet not distressed, perplexed but not in despair." You know a wonderful remedy for trouble.

The End of All Trouble Is Coming

Now a closing word. Thank God, the end of all trouble is coming soon and won't that be wonderful —the end of ills in this body? Bill, wouldn't you like to be young again? Roger, wouldn't you like to be a young man again?

Billy Carl, you old gray head here, wouldn't you like to be a young man again? (We tease Billy Carl, about his gray hair.)

Listen, one of these days there will be the end of all troubles. Won't it be wonderful to awake in His likeness? All the troubles of sin, all the troubles of disease, all the troubles of misunderstanding gone—won't it be good? Dr. H. A. Ironside was a great friend of THE SWORD OF THE LORD and wrote many sermons and sent them for publication. There came an event that brought some grief between me and Dr. Ironside because he was such a dear friend of Dr. Chafer. Dr. Chafer's book against evangelism caused a great deal of harm and I tried to get Moody Press to discontinue it and then finally exposed it publicly. And eventually they did turn it loose and turned it over to VanKampen Press and VanKampen went broke and then they turned it over to Dunham. But I started to say— between Dr. Ironside and me who had been such good friends, there came some estrangement and I was sad. But before he died he and I were together up at Minneapolis at the big summer conference at Medicine Lake and we got some good fellowship together. And he told me very proudly, "Did you know my son John is becoming an evangelist?" He was so proud! And he said other words sent from his son. I asked him to write some sermons for THE SWORD. Then he went over to Australia and New Zealand and died there and was buried there in a far-off land. But Dr. Ironside and I, I feel like we are good friends. He is on my side now and I will be on his when we see him again. And whatever the misunderstanding, it will all be gone between Christians when God will wipe away all tears from our eyes. The end of all sorrow, all trouble, all old age, all disease, all weariness, all separation, the end of the trouble is coming.

Bless God, Jesus is coming.

Will God Dwell With Men On the Earth?

(As preached at Calvary Baptist Church, Wheaton, Illinois, Christmas night, 1955.)

I. God Walked With Sinless Adam in Eden's Beauty
II. God's Shekinah Glory Dwelt in Solomon's Temple
III. God the Son Became Man to Save Men
IV. God the Spirit Now Dwells in God's Children
V. Christ Jesus Will Reign, God on David's Throne at His Second Coming
VI. God the Father Will Then Bring Heaven Down to Earth to Dwell Forever With Redeemed Men

"But will God in very deed dwell with men on the earth? behold, heaven and the heaven of heavens cannot contain thee; how much less this house which I have built."—II Chron. 6:18.

Solomon had just built the temple. It was a beautiful building, the richest building this world had ever seen till that time, taking millions of dollars' worth of gold to plate the walls of that temple and to provide the golden vessels and furniture. It was the most marvelous thing made by human hands up to that time. But Solomon, after he had made it and dedicated it to God, with a sense of dismay on him says, 'Can God dwell with men? We've built God a house, but the heaven of heavens cannot contain Him. Will God indeed dwell with men on the earth?' Now note that part of the text, "But will God in very deed dwell with men on the earth?"

You never saw a church building but what it was built with the idea that God dwells there: this is a house of God. And so it is with every altar ever built. So it is that every time anybody comes to pray we have this thought: God is on earth or near enough to hear.

It is the Christmastime now. And at the Christmas season the wonderful thought is that God sent His Son to come down to earth to become a man. In one word, a text for this sermon would be the word in Matthew 1:23 which describes Jesus, "They shall call his name Emmanuel, which being interpreted is, God with us." EMMANUEL means God dwelling on earth with men! Jesus Christ came to be with us and to dwell on the earth.

"But will God in very deed dwell with men on the earth?" I want to go back and find God's plan through the ages about God's dwelling with men on the earth, the ways God did dwell and will dwell on earth with man, from the Garden of Eden to the new heavens and the new earth.

I hope God will get some of the grandeur and the glory of it into our hearts tonight as we think about God Himself dwelling on earth.

I. God Himself Associated With Man Continually in the Garden of Eden

First of all, God came to dwell in the Garden of Eden. God was on the earth and walked up and down the paths of the garden, stopped to smell the flowers, stopped and listened to the birds, and they were not afraid. They sang and came and rested on God's hand and shoulder and looked into His clear eyes—and they sang their sweetest. All the earth was good, including man, and God was at home on the earth. There was no curse on the earth and no curse on mankind. Man and woman felt perfectly free in the presence of God. They were naked, but unashamed, pure and sinless and undefiled, and God came and walked on the earth.

There are some lessons here. First of all, this goes to show that God intended man for Himself. God made man in His image and to be His companion. Oh, man has fallen; man is an alien from God. Curses come so naturally to the tongue of a man. ". . . they go astray as soon as they be born, speaking lies" (Ps. 58:3). "Whose mouth is full of cursing and bitterness." "The way of peace have they not known" (Rom. 3:14, 17). You could go through the Bible finding text after text that shows man is not fit for God. Man is an alien from God. Man is not at home with God and so God does not live on the earth as He did before man fell. But God did live on the earth, and that goes to show that man was intended as a companion for God. I do not know why, but some way God so loved mankind and longed to have all of us with Him forever and to walk and talk with us as His dear companions and as His intimate friends and fellow workers.

So God made man, and on the earth He walked with man. On a sinful earth, on an accursed planet with nature itself under the ban, and with man himself alienated, God cannot walk now as He one time could walk on the earth with men. But God made man for Himself and this earth has not always been bad. It was good.

The foolish idea of the evolutionists that everything has just evolved by a natural process, by the war of tooth and fang and trial and error; that out of this jumble and mess and bloodshed and rapine and beasts of prey and sins of men—out of this all the animals evolved and man then developed finally—that picture that evolutionists draw of this earth is not a true picture. The true picture is that God made the world so wonderful it was fit for the paradise of God. It *was* a paradise of God. And here on earth it will be again God's paradise; will be again what it was intended to be. It will be fit for the footsteps of God on this very earth.

Look into the throats of the flowers that bloom; they are beautiful enough for God Himself to delight in. He made them. You smell their fragrance and you can know that God made them sweet for Himself. You can pluck the fruit from the trees and know that originally as God made them, they were good to the taste of God Almighty, and God looked on them and saw them good. This earth was made for God. That means in the nature of the case any kind of theology, any kind of an understanding of the Scriptures that does not bring Christ back to reign on earth with those He has redeemed to God, has fallen short. God has to have His Son come back so God can walk on this earth.

I do not wonder that Solomon asked the question, "Will God in very deed dwell with men on the earth?" He expressed the longing; he saw something of the obstacles, and said, 'The heaven of heavens itself cannot contain Him, but oh, if God would dwell with men on the earth.' I say God did dwell with man before the fall. That proves that man was made for God, proves the earth was made for God, and when they are redeemed, brought back and restored, then one day God will find the earth fit to live on and man a fit companion for God.

II. God, in the Shekinah Glory, Was on Earth During O. T. Times

But wait a minute. The Scripture makes clear here that God was on the earth in Old Testament times even in a peculiar sense, after sin came in.

Solomon, you are building a temple? You will go out of this place; the glory of the Lord will come into the temple. After they had put that altar of incense in, after they had put in those cherubims—a giant figure of a cherubim with one wing extended to the wall and the other extended to the center of the mercy seat, and the other cherubim with his wings unfolded from the other wall back to the mercy seat—then in that place there came a living, shining glory of fire and smoke; a cloud filled the temple and God Himself made Himself manifest on earth. From this time on until the temple was destroyed, until God called Nebuchadnezzar to come to bring His curse upon the city and to tear down the temple and take away the golden vessels, as far as we know, for all these years in that holy of holies in the temple there was a Shekinah glory, the presence of God Himself.

That is the same presence of God that Moses saw in the burning bush that burned and was not consumed out on the back side of the desert of Midian where Moses kept the sheep. That same fire was God on earth, and God spoke to Moses out of the bush and said, 'My name is I AM. Go tell Pharaoh that I AM has sent thee. I am the God of Abraham and Isaac and Jacob.' God was on earth in that fire.

Then Moses led the children of Israel out and, strangely, the manifest presence of God was seen there. In the daytime there was a pillar of cloud reaching up into the sky, the presence of God, and it led and they followed. When the night came on, that pillar of cloud became a pillar of fire through the night.

You may drive along the highway in West Texas on out toward El Paso, and if you drive in the night, yonder there is a flaming fire shooting a hundred or two hundred feet into the air. It is a burning gas well. How it reminds you of the way it must have looked for a hundred miles around all the camp of Israel as they saw the flaming fire of God, the literal presence of God on earth. And when the pillar of fire or cloud moved, then the children of Israel got ready and the priests took up their burdens, and the Levites carried the tabernacle and the instruments, and they marched. Judah in the forefront—and God was with them. Then when the pillar of fire halted, they halted too, and there they made their camp.

It was that fire that was the fire on the altar. When Moses had completed the tabernacle and the great brazen altar, and the offerings were brought for the first sacrifice, God said, 'Bring no fire, Moses. I'll furnish the fire.' But the two worldly minded, reckless sons of the high priest Aaron, Nadab and Abihu, went to a campfire and shoveled up some coals and put them down on the altar to build a fire, and God struck them dead. When some of the people would have mourned, God told Moses, 'Tell them no mourning. No mourning. I'll strike them dead, too.' Not a tear to be shed. Not a bit of mourning for those who neglected, ignored, and scorned the living God in putting their own fire on the altar there.

It was the same fire of God, the presence of God, that came and burned down Sodom and Gomorrah. That was the living fire burning with brimstone that destroyed those cities—the literal presence of God on earth.

It was that same fire that Elijah called down on the captain and his fifty men. Elijah was on a hilltop and the captain said, 'Thou man of God, come down.' Elijah said, "If I be a man of God, let fire come down from heaven, and consume thee and thy fifty."

Oh, the fearful God! If God is going to dwell with men, and men be such sinners, and God is so furious at sin—why, the fire will come to destroy, and it leads only to Hell! If God lives in the Shekinah glory; God in the burning bush; God on the flaming altar; God in the vengeance that comes from sin; oh, then it all leads up to the fire and brimstone of Hell. O God! If You are to dwell on earth, You must do something more; there must be some way to buy back man and make man fit for God to dwell on the earth. "But will God in very deed dwell with men on the earth?"

Oh, then if God is going to dwell peaceably with men on the earth, He has to come some other way.

III. God Made Flesh to Dwell Among Men: Christ Comes

So God made His plans, and one day down the stately steps of the stairway from the skies yonder God the Creator came and lodged in the womb of a virgin. And Jehovah God of the Old Testament became Emmanuel, "God with us." Yonder at the season we represent by our Christmas, a Baby was born of a virgin and laid in a manger, and God had come to the earth in the person of His own Son—not just a man, Jesus, upon whom came a spirit, as the Christian Scientists say, "the Spirit of the Christ," and as Nels Ferre and the modernists and the Barthians say, "God's Agape." No, God Almighty Himself, God became flesh. "The Word was made flesh, and dwelt among us, (and we beheld his glory, the glory as of the only begotten of the Father,) . . ." God came to dwell with men.

Jesus, you remember, the night He was betrayed, laid aside His garments and girded Himself with a towel and took a pan of water and washed the disciples' feet. Oh, but there is a glory in the phrase, He "laid aside his garments." That is not the first time. He laid aside in Heaven that garment which He wore for a bit on the Mount of Transfiguration, t h a t garment which was as "white as the light" and "his face did shine as the sun." He had laid aside the glory of the Creator and the manifestation of the eternal God Himself. As John saw Him in Revelation, His feet were "like unto fine brass, as if they burned in a furnace," and His face was too bright for a mortal man to look upon it, and John fell at His feet as dead. He laid aside that outward glory and became a man, a baby nursed at a woman's breast. He learned to talk; He went up to the temple when His mother and Joseph went. He was subject to His mother and His foster father, and so grew to manhood. At thirty years, He had never preached a sermon. Thirty years old, and He had never won a soul, never opened a blind eye, never manifested any of His glory. Then one day He came to John in Jordan and, as our example, He was baptized. And behold, the Spirit of God came upon Him, and He entered into that marvelous ministry. He raised the dead, healed the sick; opened blind eyes, cured the lepers, saved the sinner, made the harlot pure, made the drunkard sober. Oh, God among men, Emmanuel!

But do you know how that turned out? This world hated Him. "He came unto his own, and his own received him not"—God Himself in the flesh. Now men already hated God, but they could never spit on God until Jesus was in Pilate's judgment hall and there they came by and got Him by the beard and pulled out handsful of

151

beard and spit in His face. Men hated God, but they never before had a chance to tie a rag around His face and blindfold Him and then hit Him over the head and say, 'Now tell who hit You, King of the Jews! Come on, prophesy who hit You.' Men never before had a chance to gnash on God with their teeth and to slander Him and abuse Him, and when He was thirsty to rub vinegar and gall on the parched lips instead of water, and to nail Him to a cross with felons. Man up to that time had never gotten to show what man really thought about God and how man felt about God until God became a Man and dwelt on earth. But one day He died, and the sky turned black, the sun did not shine, and even God turned His face away. I say, "Why, why, O God, why?"

And God answers back, 'If God is to dwell with man, the debt of sin must be paid and men must be redeemed and men must be bought back.'

"Why the crown of thorns pressed down on the Saviour?"

And He says, 'Nature must be redeemed, too, and I am going to have to kill and cure the thorns of this world and the sting of the mosquitoes and the thorns on the roses and the plague of drouth on the prairies when there is no rain and the tumultuous hurricanes that destroy and the storms at sea and the enmity in every beast of prey.' And God says, 'I am going to have to kill the thorns and let Jesus die with a crown of thorns.' God is come to live on this earth in Jesus. Then they brought Him down from the cross and buried Him. But He rose again from the grave.

IV. The Blessed Holy Spirit Now Lives on Earth in Bodies of God's Children

But wait, let us go back to the last night—the last night when Jesus called His disciples around Him. He knew He was going to be crucified the next day and He said to them, "Let not your heart be troubled."

But they said, 'We are troubled.'

He said, 'I'm going away.'

They said, 'Don't go! Jesus. Don't go! You mustn't go.'

'Yes,' Jesus said, 'I'm going. It's better for you that I go.'

'How could it be better? What will we do without you?'

And Jesus answered, 'If I go away, I'll send the Comforter to you.'

And so now we come to the next phase of God's dwelling on earth. Solomon asked God, "Will God in very deed dwell with men on the earth?" Jesus said, 'I'm going back to the Father.' They went out one day, out there to the Mount of Olivet and Jesus gave His last command, the Great Commission, and He breathed on them and blessed them and then, up, up, up He went and a cloud received Him out of their sight, and Jesus was gone. But two men (angels) stood by in white apparel and said, 'Don't think that's the last, men of Galilee. This same Jesus shall so come in like manner.' 'But meantime,' they thought, 'what will we do without God on earth while Jesus is gone and before

His kingdom comes? What will we do?'

But Jesus had said, 'I'll send you a Comforter.' And the blessed Comforter came in His place. The blessed Comforter! Now then; is He God? Yes, God the Holy Spirit. But that is not all. Jesus said, 'If a man love me, he will keep my commandments, and I will come and manifest myself to him.

They said, 'How will you manifest yourself to us and not to the world, Jesus?'

He said, 'The Comforter, which is the Holy Ghost, which is with you and shall be in you, He will come, and my Father and I will both manifest ourselves unto you.' That is the reason the Holy Spirit is sometimes called the Holy Spirit, sometimes is called the Spirit of God who represents God the Father, and sometimes is called the Spirit of Christ for He represents Christ and He is "Christ in you, the hope of glory." Every saved person has God inside. My body—I ought not to defile it! My body—I ought to take good care of it! My body—this mind, every thought it has; these eyes, everything they see; these ears, everything they hear; these hands, everything they do; these feet, everywhere I go—God dwells in this body! God does not dwell in church houses. He dwells not in temples made with hands, but God dwells in the bodies of Christians. "What? know ye not that your body is the temple of the Holy Ghost which is in you, which ye have of God, and ye are not your own? For ye are bought with a price: therefore glorify God in your body, and in your spirit, which are God's" (I Cor. 6:19, 20). So God now dwells in the bodies of Christians.

You know, it is wonderful. "Lo, I am with you alway," Jesus said.

I've seen the lightning flashing,
I've heard the thunder roll,
I've felt sin's breakers dashing,
Trying to conquer my soul.
I've heard the voice of my Saviour
Bidding me still to fight on;
He promised never to leave me,
Never to leave me alone.

Ah, thank God, the blessed Holy Spirit has come!

O spread the tidings 'round,
Wherever man is found,
Wherever human hearts and human woes abound;
Let ev'ry Christian tongue
Proclaim the joyful sound:
The Comforter has come!

The blessed Holy Spirit is God in you and God in me.

One may think, Wouldn't it be wonderful if God would dwell with men? Oh, if God would come down; if God were not far off and I could have His fellowship; if I could have His fellowship as John did at the supper table when he moved his couch over near and laid his head on the breast of Jesus. If I could have fellowship, if my doubts were as easy to settle as when doubting Thomas said, 'If I could only put my fingers in His hands, and put my hand in His side, and see for myself and be sure it's Jesus risen from the dead.' And Jesus said 'You can. Come on, Thomas, you can see.

Oh, if Jesus were present like that!

But He is! Blessed be God—God with you, God on earth!

"But will God in very deed dwell with men on the earth?" Yes, God the Holy Spirit, and through Him, Christ the Son, and through Him, God the Father, dwell in my body. I can read the Bible and say, "Blessed God, explain it." And He does. And I can say, "Blessed God, what shall I do?" and He tells me.

I was going to fly one day to Minneapolis for a board meeting of Northwestern Schools. I had so much to do, but I felt maybe I ought to go. I sent a letter to Dr. Billy Graham, then president of the schools, and said, "If you need me, I'll come, but if you don't need me, please let me know. I'm so busy. I don't mind spending fifty or sixty dollars for the trip, but if you don't need me, let me know in time." No word came and I started to go from Wheaton to the Chicago airport, twenty-six miles away. I got in my car. I drove eight miles down the road, and I stopped the car and said to my wife, "I'm not going. I'm not going. I'm not needed."

She said, "How do you know?"

I said, "God just tells me I'm not needed. I'm not going." I turned around and drove back home.

My son-in-law, Walt Handford, came over and said, "Did you get the telegram?"

I said, "What telegram?"

He said, "Didn't they page you at the airport?"

I said, "No. I never did get to the airport."

"Well," he said, "You got a telegram from Dr. Billy Graham saying that it was a routine meeting, and you didn't need to come."

You know, we can have God with us. Miracle of miracles, we can have God Himself with us. We can ask Him questions. We can know which way to go. We can have wisdom. We can understand the Scriptures. Oh, God with us! It is amazing!

V. But God Must Come to Rule in Christ's Second Coming

"But will God in very deed dwell with men on the earth?" In some sense, He does in the indwelling of the blessed Spirit of God now. Oh yes, it's true in us who are Christians. But this world is someway out of joint, and the more spiritual the Christian, the less he fits in this world. "This world is not my home, I'm just passing through." We are strangers, sojourners, and pilgrims. Yes, I know I can have God in the blessed Holy Spirit, but this world does not know God. The governments are not in the hands of God. The education and philosophy of this world do not represent God. The United Nations does not represent God. Public sentiment, the vote of the people, does not represent God. Does God dwell on earth? Yes, in the hearts and lives of some people. But that is not enough. That is not as it was in the Garden of Eden when God indeed dwelt with men on the earth. That is not enough.

Wait a minute—it is not done! It isn't done, blessed be God! One of these days it will be as the angel who stood by said, 'Yes, I know you saw Him go, but this same Jesus shall so come in like manner as you've seen Him go into Heaven.' "In like manner"; He will come in the clouds. "In like manner"; His feet will stand on the Mount of Olives. Yes, and the book of Zechariah tells us that the earthquake caused by His feet touching the earth will split the mountain from east to west and from it will flow out a river. Oh, I say, He is coming! He is coming! Then what will happen? You talk about the governments of the earth; you talk about a United Nations assembly where a traitor, Alger Hiss, can go to help give away our liberties and all the people are ashamed to stop to pray and call on Almighty God lest they insult the Soviet Union. You talk about a United Nation where all countries want us for the billions we give away and they despise us for our religion, and even we are poor enough, God knows. But wait! One of these days He will come and there will be the shout and the voice of the archangel and the dead in Christ shall rise. Then a little later, He will come riding upon a white horse and He will be crowned with many crowns, and the heavens will split and we will see the sign of the Son of Man. He will come back. He will come—Ah, with the army of Heaven. And the Lord Jesus will take up His rightful place.

Not now the meek and lowly Jesus, not now the Lamb of God! Now He comes the Lion of the tribe of Judah. First He came to shed His own blood, but now He is coming to shed the blood of His enemies. Before, His garments were stripped off and the blood dripped down His side and ran off His feet and formed a pool below the cross: but this time His garments will be red with blood, the blood of His enemies at the Battle of Armageddon. Then Christ will set up His throne. He is the Stone without hands cut out of the mountain. He is the one that shall smite the great statue representing the kingdoms of this world. And, bless God, in a moment there will be no more United States government, there will be no more British Empire, there will be no more Soviet Union, there will be no more "People's Republic," in China. But Jesus Christ will take the kingdoms of this world and He will be King of kings and Lord of lords.

Handel's Hallelujah Chorus from *The Messiah* gives a little foretaste of it. And when Handel had written it, he said, "I did think that Heaven itself was opened and Jesus was coming." Well, Handel, one of these days you will see it and hear it, and the angels and the saints will rejoice and say, "The Lord God omnipotent reigneth," when Christ shall come to the earth and set up His throne and reign on the earth! That will be a good thing, won't it? A good thing!

Praise the Lord, Jesus Christ Himself is coming back to reign on the earth and it will be God *on a throne!* Not God in a manger in a stable, but God *on a throne!* Not God on a cross with spittle on His face and Him bruised and beaten and His beard plucked out, and Him so marred that He does not look like a man. But He will be God on a throne, God giving the orders then, God ruling the world when the kingdoms of earth are become the kingdom of our Lord and of His Christ!

"But will God in very deed dwell with men on the earth?" Yes, thank God. And Jesus will come and reign on the throne of His father, David. Isaiah, chapter eleven tells us a little about that blessed time when the Lord Jesus comes back to reign. Listen to these words:

"And there shall come forth a rod out of the stem of Jesse, and a Branch shall grow out of his roots: And the spirit of the Lord shall rest upon him, the spirit of wisdom and understanding, the spirit of counsel and might, the spirit of knowledge and of the fear of the Lord; And shall make him of quick understanding in the fear of the Lord: and he shall not judge after the sight of his eyes, neither reprove after the hearing of his ears: But with righteousness shall he judge the poor, and reprove with equity for the meek of the earth: and he shall smite the earth with the rod of his mouth, and with the breath of his lips shall he slay the wicked. And righteousness shall be the girdle of his loins, and faithfulness the girdle of his reins. The wolf also shall dwell with the lamb."

What! On this accursed earth that brings forth thorns and thistles and where men can only grow a crop with sweat and toil and disappointment? This earth is plagued by locusts and plagued by hurricanes and plagued by fire and flood and the stings of insects and disease germs. It is going to be changed. "And the leopard shall lie down with the kid; and the calf and the young lion and the fatling together." And a little child can go out and lead the calf around or the lion around or the lamb or the leopard or the wolf. It would not matter. He can handle all of them.

"And the cow and the bear shall feed; their young ones shall lie down together: and the lion shall eat straw like the ox. And the sucking child shall play on the hole of the asp, and the weaned child shall put his hand on the cockatrice' den. They shall not hurt nor destroy in all my holy mountain: for the earth shall be full of the knowledge of the Lord, as the waters cover the sea."

Oh, when Jesus was born in Bethlehem, that was just the start. We have not seen the glorious finale. We will when He comes to reign again.

And then what? Listen! Then the Scripture says, in Isaiah 35:1, 2, 5-8, 10:

"The wilderness and the solitary place shall be glad for them; and the desert shall rejoice, and blossom as the rose. It shall blossom abundantly . . . Then the eyes of the blind shall be opened, and the ears of the deaf shall be unstopped. Then shall the lame man leap as an hart, and the tongue of the dumb sing: for in the wilderness shall waters break out, and streams in the desert. And the parched ground shall become a pool, and the thirsty land springs

of water ... And an highway shall be there, and a way, and it shall be called the way of holiness ... And the ransomed of the Lord shall return, and come to Zion with songs and everlasting joy upon their heads: they shall obtain joy and gladness, and sorrow and sighing shall flee away."

Praise God!

"But will God in very deed dwell with men on the earth?" Yes, Jesus will return to reign on the earth.

VI. Then God the Father Will Make Heaven on Earth and Dwell With Men Forever!

But that is not the end of the story. He will come back to reign, oh yes, but wait just a minute. He will reign for a thousand years. It will go like a song of joy. How blessed to plow the ground when there is never a weed to bother! How blessed to sow the seed when every seed brings forth fruit! How blessed to grow when there's rain always in season. How blessed to preach when everybody believes what you preach! How blessed to sing when there is never a note out of tune! How blessed the life with loved ones when everybody agrees with you. How blessed it will be when there is no more goodbye, no parting, no cemetery, no funeral, no sickness, no old age, no eyeglasses, no gray hair. Praise the Lord!

And then when Jesus Christ has licked the whole thing and when the just period of probation has proven that God Himself is the only remedy for sin, then one day the Son will turn the kingdom over to the Father and God Himself in His fullness, God the Father, God Almighty, not only Jesus the Son but God the Father will come down to the earth. I will read you the story over in Revelation 21: 1-4: "And I saw a new heaven" This is at the end of the thousand years. The last sinners have been purged out. The Great White Throne Judgment is over. The last rebellion is done, and now, "I saw a new heaven and a new earth." God is going to make the earth new. Every mark left by battlefields, all the thorns and thistles and plagues and germs will be gone, and a new Garden of Eden it will be. And there will be the trees of life bearing the twelve manner of fruit, and there will be the leaves for the eternal healing of the nations. And then, the Scripture says,

"The first heaven and the first earth were passed away; and there was no more sea. [We will need all the land at that time for people to live on, there will be so many saints of God here.] And I John saw the holy city, new Jerusalem, coming down from God out of heaven, prepared as a bride adorned for her husband. And I heard a great voice out of heaven saying, Behold, the tabernacle of God is with men, and he will dwell with them, and they shall be his people, and God himself shall be with them, and be their God. And God shall wipe away all tears from their eyes: and there shall be no more death, neither sorrow, nor crying, neither shall there be any more pain: for the former things are passed away."

God Himself will dwell literally, eternally on the earth. Sun! You can quit your shining; you're just a little candle God put out there for a little season for a darkened planet gone away from God! We will not need you then, for the Lord God will be the light then. Praise the Lord! Praise the Lord! Cemeteries—no good now! The bones are all out and the bodies have been resurrected. The saved are here, and those lost are gone on to Hell. We won't need the cemeteries; throw down the stones. Hospitals—well, you can turn them into pavilions for joy and laughter and music and friendship. No more hospitals, praise God! Doctors, you will all have to have some other trade, blessed be God! Yes sir, you won't bury any more mistakes then, doctors, when God comes to dwell on the earth eternally with men. And babies can play with roses and there will be no thorns then. Babies can play with snakes then, and "they shall not hurt nor destroy in all my holy mountain." And then they shall say, "Let us go up into the house of the Lord." God Himself is the light and the new Jerusalem, Heavenly City itself, is come down to earth and Heaven is on earth because God is on earth. God Himself shall dwell with men.

The Only Way to Dwell With God Is to Let Christ Into Your Heart

Now these closing words. Yes, God meant to dwell on earth, and bless God, He will. But first you must have Him in your heart or you won't dwell with Him. That's right.

At the heart's door, the Saviour's waiting,
At the heart's door, fast closed by sin.
Don't you hear Him gently knocking?
Draw the bolt, and let Him in.

Jesus says, "Behold, I stand at the door, and knock: if any man hear my voice, and open the door, I will come in to him, and will sup with him, and he with me" (Rev. 3:20).

Ah, bless God, you can have God go home with you tonight in your heart.

I was out in Waterloo, Iowa, and a man made a casting and gave it to me. It was a door knocker, beautifully cast, and it said, "God dwells within." That is only partly true. God dwells in my heart, but bless God, one day God will dwell on earth with men. I look forward to the fulfillment when God will dwell with us on the earth. Man was made for that. Earth was made for that. All the trees and mountains and flowers and animals were made for a perfect, holy God to dwell among and for man who was to be His dearest companion and constant joy. One day, God will have His way.

Then this glad word of Solomon, "But will God in very deed dwell with men on the earth?" Yes, God will. Yes, God will

Dear sinner friend, you have read the above sermon. You know you are a poor, unconverted, lost sinner. The only way you can ever live with God is to turn from sin to let Jesus Christ come into your heart. If you will, you may open the door of your heart. He died to save you. He is ready. He waits now for you to confess your sinful need and trust Him to come in, to forgive, to save.

The new year has already begun. If you are ever to be saved, it is time now. Today, I beg you, open your heart to Jesus, trust Him, claim Him as your Saviour today!

To make it easy, I put the decision below for you. Will you honestly say yes to God, sign this statement sincerely, then copy it in a letter and mail it to me today? Oh, do it now; let Jesus Christ come in to dwell forever, to forgive and save. Sign it, mean it, and copy and mail it right now, I beg you!

Evangelist John R. Rice,
Editor, The Sword of the Lord,
214 W. Wesley,
Wheaton, Illinois.

Dear Brother Rice:

I have read your sermon, *"Will God Dwell With Men on the Earth."* I realize I am a poor, lost sinner. But I believe Jesus Christ died to pay for my sins and to save my soul. He has promised to save all who trust Him. This moment, with all my heart, I do trust Him to forgive me and save my soul. I depend on Him to come into my heart to stay. I will claim Him openly as my Saviour and will set out to live for Him as my Lord.

Here is my solemn signature, claiming Christ as my own Saviour.

Signed _____

Address _____

_____